Quietly Confident:

How Introverts Can Excel in a World That Can't Stop Talking

FIRST EDITION

I0479420

Dr. Lila McKenzie

Publisher's Note

The information contained within this book is based on the author's research, experiences, and opinions. The author and publisher have made every effort to ensure accuracy and completeness, but make no warranties or guarantees regarding the information provided. Readers are encouraged to exercise their own judgment and seek professional advice where necessary. The publisher, author, and any other involved parties cannot be held liable for any errors or omissions in the content.

First published in the United States in 2023 by ByteWise Publishing.

ISBNs

Kindle edition   N/A
Paperback edition   9798388458117

THIS PAGE IS INTENTIONALLY LEFT BLANK

Table of Contents

Chapter 2: The Science of Introversion: Unraveling the Mysteries 32

Chapter 3: Myth-Busting: Debunking Introvert Stereotypes and Misconceptions 53

Chapter 4: Quiet Power: Identifying and Leveraging Your Unique Introverted Strengths — 71

Chapter 5: Communication Mastery: Introvert-Friendly Strategies for Effective Interaction 92

Chapter 6: Networking for Introverts: Building Connections Without Burning Out 114

Chapter 7: Thriving in an Extroverted World: Navigating Social and Professional Landscapes 135

Chapter 8: The Introverted Leader: Harnessing Your Quiet Strengths for Effective Leadership 156

Chapter 9: Personal Growth: Fostering Confidence, Resilience, and Self-Acceptance 177

Chapter 10: Conclusion: The Journey Continues – Your Path to an Empowered Introverted Life 198

About the author

Dr. Lila McKenzie is a renowned introvert advocate, psychologist, and international speaker. With over 20 years of experience working with introverted clients, she has honed her expertise in helping them unlock their unique potential and thrive in a world dominated by extroverted ideals. Dr. McKenzie holds a Ph.D. in Psychology from Yale University and is a regular contributor to major publications like The New York Times, Forbes, and Psychology Today. As an introvert herself, she understands firsthand the struggles and strengths of introverted individuals and has dedicated her career to empowering introverts around the world.

THIS PAGE IS INTENTIONALLY LEFT BLANK

Chapter 1: Introduction: Embracing Your Introverted Nature

The Power of Introversion – Understanding the Inner World of Introverts

The Quiet Revolution – Rise of the Introvert Culture

The world has always celebrated the qualities of extroversion. It is the outgoing and assertive qualities that we have been conditioned to admire in people, be it in social, work, or academic situations. But in recent times, there has been a shift towards celebrating introversion. The Quiet Revolution, as it is called, has brought about a change in societal perception towards introverts.

One of the strongest examples of this shift took place in 2012 when Susan Cain's book, Quiet: The Power of Introverts in a World That Can't Stop Talking was published. Overnight, Cain became a sensation, and her work became a rallying cry for introverts seeking validation.

Cain's research and the subsequent research of others have shown that introverts possess unique strengths and abilities that go beyond their perceived limitations. Introverts are thoughtful, strategic, and reflective individuals who bring immense value to the world.

In this subsection, we'll explore the roots of the Quiet Revolution, the cultural shift towards embracing introversion, and the impact it has had on our society. We will also shed light on why introverts have been historically overlooked and misunderstood, and how this has resulted in an introvert-unfriendly world.

Introversion is Not a Weakness – Embracing Your True Nature

Many introverts have grown up with the belief that their quieter, more reserved nature is a disadvantage in the world. They may have been told to speak up more or to be more outgoing, leading them to believe that extroverted qualities are necessary for success. However, introversion is not a weakness, and the traits associated with being introverted can actually be strengths when properly understood and harnessed.

One of the most significant gifts of introversion is the capacity for introspection and contemplation, which allows us to tap into our deepest feelings and insights. Introverts often approach life in a more thoughtful and meaningful way, taking the time to observe and understand the world on a deeper level. This capacity for reflection also makes introverts great listeners, which enables them to truly connect with others and understand their needs.

Embracing your introverted nature means accepting yourself for who you are and recognizing that your unique qualities are what make you strong. It also means understanding that introverted traits are equally valuable in both personal and professional settings. By accepting and leveraging our introverted nature, we open ourselves up to new opportunities and greater fulfillment in life.

Common Traits of Introverts – Recognizing Your Own Qualities

Introverts share common attributes that can lead to self-understanding, acceptance, and growth. Do you enjoy solitude, introspection, and deep conversations? Are you a good listener, observant, and reflective? You may be an introvert, and recognizing your natural tendencies and strengths is the first step in embracing your introverted nature.

Introverts prefer peaceful environments and tend to avoid noisy or overly stimulating situations, as they drain their energy. They may also avoid small talk and have a preference for meaningful, one-on-one interactions. As a result, they may be mistaken for shy or anti-social, but they simply thrive on quality over quantity. They typically need time to recharge and process their thoughts and emotions before engaging in social activities again.

Introverts often excel at creative and analytical pursuits that require focus and concentration. They are keen observers and have a knack for noticing details that others may miss. They tend to be deep thinkers and feelers, and may also have a heightened sense of empathy and compassion. Many introverts also possess a rich inner world and a vivid imagination, which can lead to artistic expression or intellectual pursuits.

Knowing your introverted traits can help you leverage your

strengths and accept your limitations. It can also aid in better self-care and communication with others, as you learn to express your needs and preferences without feeling guilty or ashamed. Recognizing your common qualities as an introvert is the first step in embracing your introverted nature with confidence and pride.

The Misunderstood Introvert – Debunking Common Myths and Stereotypes

Despite the increasing awareness of introversion, many people still hold misconceptions about what it truly means to be an introvert. In this section, we will explore some of the most common myths and stereotypes and provide evidence to debunk them.

Myth 1: Introverts are shy and antisocial.
Contrary to popular belief, not all introverts are shy or antisocial. While some introverts may exhibit these characteristics, they do not define introversion as a whole. In fact, many introverts enjoy socializing and have a strong desire to connect with others on a deeper level.

Myth 2: Introverts don't like people.
This myth perpetuates the perception that introverts are misanthropes and don't enjoy being around others. However, research shows that introverts do like people and can be highly empathetic and compassionate. They just prefer more meaningful interactions and may become drained by superficial small talk.

Myth 3: Introverts are not good leaders.
Introverts can be highly effective leaders, and some of the

most successful and innovative leaders throughout history have been introverted. Unlike extroverts who may lead through charisma and social dominance, introverted leaders often lead through careful thought and decision-making, and by cultivating a loyal and motivated team.

Myth 4: Introverts need to change to succeed in the workplace.
The reality is that introverts can thrive in the workplace if they are allowed to work in ways that suit their personality. Telling introverts to "be more outgoing" or "speak up more often" can be counterproductive and lead to disengagement or burnout. By respecting and valuing the unique strengths of introverts, companies can create a more diverse and productive work environment.

By dispelling these myths and understanding the truly complex nature of introversion, we can begin to appreciate and embrace the power of introverted traits and behaviors.

The Quiet Confidence – Harnessing the Power of Your Strengths

As introverts, we often feel overshadowed by the loudness of the world around us. However, it is important to understand that we possess a unique set of skills that allow us to excel in our quiet nature. By embracing our introverted nature, we can begin to recognize the power that lies within.

Our introverted nature allows us to be excellent observers, deep thinkers, and skilled problem solvers. We have the ability to think through complex issues and come up with creative solutions. This trait is often undervalued in a world that values extroverted qualities such as being outgoing and talkative. However, introverts can harness their strengths to become quietly confident in their abilities.

By recognizing the value in our introverted nature, we can begin to build the confidence necessary to succeed. It is not a weakness to be quiet or reserved, but rather a unique aspect of our personalities that can be used to our advantage. Through quiet confidence, we can embrace our natural abilities and abilities in a world that cannot stop talking.

The journey to embracing our introverted nature may not be easy, as societal pressures and stereotypes can make it challenging to feel confident in ourselves. However, by focusing on our strengths and harnessing the power of quiet confidence, we can begin to thrive in all areas of our lives.

The Challenges of Living as an Introvert – Conquering Negative Thoughts and Behaviors

Overcoming Social Anxiety – Coping Strategies for Introverts

Social anxiety can be a real challenge for introverts. The fear of judgment and criticism, along with the pressure to conform to social norms, can be overwhelming. However, by practicing some coping strategies, introverts can overcome their social anxiety and live a fulfilling life.

One coping strategy is to prepare yourself before social events. This can involve setting clear goals for the event, such as meeting a certain number of new people or engaging in a meaningful conversation. Preparing topics of conversation beforehand can also help ease anxiety.

Another strategy is to redefine success in social situations. Instead of focusing on how many people you meet or how many conversations you have, measure success by the quality of your interactions rather than the quantity.

It's important to also remember that taking breaks during social events is perfectly acceptable. Introverts may need to retreat to a quiet space to recharge, and this is not a failure. Communicating your needs to others can also help, as friends and family can be a great support system.

Lastly, practicing mindfulness and deep breathing can be effective in calming anxiety. Being present in the moment can help quiet negative thoughts and reduce anxiety.

Conquering social anxiety is not an overnight process, but by practicing coping strategies, introverts can turn social events into enjoyable experiences.

Taming the Inner Critic – Busting the Perfectionism Trap

The Challenges of Living as an Introvert – Conquering Negative Thoughts and Behaviors
As an introvert, you may have an inner voice that is always critical of your actions. This voice often leads to a tendency towards perfectionism, which can be detrimental to your well-being. The fear of making mistakes or not performing to the highest possible standard can hold you back from taking risks and trying new things.

In this section, we will explore the roots of perfectionism and provide practical strategies for managing your inner critic. You will learn to identify the difference between healthy striving for excellence and the destructive pursuit of perfection. We will also discuss how to reframe your mindset and reprogram your inner voice to be more positive.

By learning to conquer your perfectionism and quieting your inner critic, you can free yourself from unnecessary stress and anxiety. This will open up new opportunities for personal growth and allow you to pursue your goals with a sense of ease and confidence.

Building Healthy Relationships – Trust, Boundaries and Fulfilling Connections

Introverts often struggle with building and maintaining relationships due to their innate nature of preferring solitude and introspection. However, relationships are an essential part of life, and it is crucial for introverts to learn how to build healthy and fulfilling connections while still honoring their need for solitude.

One of the most critical aspects of building relationships as an introvert is trust. Introverts tend to be private people who do not easily open up to others. Therefore, it is essential to build trust with people before sharing personal thoughts and feelings. Trust can be built by starting with small disclosures and gradually increasing the level of vulnerability over time.

Another vital aspect of building relationships as an introvert is setting boundaries. Introverts need to take care of their energy levels and set boundaries with people who drain them. This might mean saying no to social events or limiting the time spent with particular people. It is essential to communicate these boundaries clearly and assertively to avoid misunderstandings and hurt feelings.

Finally, fulfilling connections require an understanding of the unique needs of introverts. Introverts thrive in one-on-one conversations rather than group settings, so it's essential to cultivate deep and meaningful connections with a few close friends rather than trying to have many shallow relationships. Introverts may also prefer non-traditional means of communication, such as writing letters or having phone conversations. Understanding these nuances can help introverts build relationships that are both meaningful and fulfilling.

Emotional Intelligence for Introverts – Navigating Conflicts and Stressful Situations

Introverts are often perceived as emotionally reserved or distant, but this is far from the truth. Introverts often have the same range and intensity of emotions as extroverts, but they express and process them differently. Understanding emotional intelligence can help introverts navigate conflicts and stressful situations with ease and confidence.

Emotional intelligence involves the ability to recognize and manage one's own emotions, as well as understand and empathize with the emotions of others. Introverts can cultivate emotional intelligence by learning to recognize their own emotions and triggers, and developing strategies for managing them.

One powerful tool for introverts is mindfulness meditation, which involves paying attention to the present moment without judgment. Mindfulness can help introverts become more aware of their emotions and regulate them more effectively, reducing stress and enhancing overall well-being.

Another valuable skill for introverts is communication, especially in challenging situations. Rather than avoiding conflicts, introverts can learn to communicate assertively and actively listen, expressing themselves clearly and advocating for their own needs while still respecting others' perspectives.

It's important for introverts to honor their own emotional needs, setting healthy boundaries and avoiding overstimulation. This can involve taking breaks when necessary, avoiding toxic or draining relationships, and creating a supportive and empowering daily routine.

By mastering emotional intelligence, introverts can navigate the challenges of living in an extroverted world with confidence and grace, harnessing their unique strengths and abilities to achieve success and personal fulfillment.

Self-Care for Introverts – Practices for Maintaining Balance and Inner Peace

As an introvert, you may face challenges in your daily life that are unique to your inner world. While it's normal to feel drained after social interactions, introverts are prone to negative thoughts and behaviors that can be detrimental to their health and well-being. In this section, we will explore the challenges of living as an introvert and provide practical tips for conquering negative thoughts and behaviors.

As an introvert, it's important to prioritize self-care and maintain a healthy balance between social interactions and alone time. Here are some practices that can help you maintain inner peace and avoid burnout:

Take Breaks – If you feel overwhelmed during social interactions, find a quiet space to take a break and recharge your batteries. Even a few minutes of solitude can help you regain your energy and focus.

Practice Mindfulness – Mindfulness meditation is a

powerful tool for introverts to cultivate inner peace and reduce stress. Focus on your breath and observe your thoughts without judgment.

Set Boundaries – It's okay to say no to social invitations or requests that don't align with your values or priorities. Setting clear boundaries is essential for introverts to maintain their well-being.

Embrace Solo Activities – Engage in activities that bring you joy and don't require social interaction, such as reading, writing, or exercising. These activities can help you recharge your batteries and improve your mood.

Cultivate Gratitude – Gratitude is a powerful mindset that can help introverts focus on the positive aspects of their life and foster inner peace. Take a few minutes each day to appreciate the things you're thankful for.

By prioritizing self-care and practicing these techniques, introverts can conquer negative thoughts and behaviors and lead a more balanced and empowered life.

Empowering Your Inner Introvert – Identifying Your Purpose and Motivations

Discovering Your Passions – Identifying Your Unique Talents and Strengths

As an introvert, it's easy to feel like an outsider in a world that celebrates extroverted qualities such as assertiveness, confidence and extraversion. But the truth is, being an introvert is not a weakness, and it's entirely possible to thrive as an introvert by understanding and embracing your unique strengths and talents.

One of the keys to unlocking your full potential as an introvert is to identify your passions and motivators. These are the things that give you energy and bring you joy, and by tapping into them, you can increase your sense of fulfillment and purpose.

To begin discovering your passions, take an inventory of your skills, interests, and natural talents. What comes easily to you? What do you enjoy doing? What have others complimented you on in the past? These can all be clues to your unique strengths and talents.

Another helpful exercise is to reflect on the moments when you've felt most alive and fulfilled. What were you doing at those times? Who were you with? What was it about those experiences that made them so meaningful to you? This kind of introspection can help you identify your passions and motivations and give you the direction you need to pursue them more fully.

Remember, identifying your passions and strengths is just the first step in empowering your inner introvert. In the following sections, we'll explore strategies for leveraging these strengths to achieve your goals and thrive in a world that often values extroverted qualities over introverted ones.

Creating a Life that Aligns with Your Values – Finding Meaning and Purpose in Your Work and Personal Life

As an introvert, the first step to embracing your nature is understanding your purpose and motivation. You need to identify the things that bring you joy and fulfillment. This, in turn, will enable you to create a life that aligns with your values, which is an essential component to feeling empowered in your introverted nature.

The first step towards this journey is finding meaning and purpose in your work life. Oftentimes, it can be difficult to find a job that is aligned with your values as an introvert. However, research shows that people who align their work with their values are more productive and have higher job satisfaction. Therefore, it is important to assess the nature of the job and the workplace environment before making a commitment.

Another way to empower your inner introvert is through your personal life. This means identifying the relationships and activities that are meaningful to you. For introverts, it is crucial to have alone time and recharge their social battery. Hence, identifying the right people, hobbies, and activities that allow you to recharge are critical to your overall well-being.

Ultimately, finding purpose and motivation for introverts means taking a step back and assessing the things that bring you joy and fulfillment. Identifying these will allow you to create a life that is aligned with your values and motivations, enabling you to thrive in the world as an empowered introvert.

Mindful Living – Bringing Awareness and Intentionality to Your Daily Routine

As an introvert, the way you live your life matters just as much as what you do with it. Mindful living can help you understand what matters to you and create a daily routine aligned with your values and long-term goals.
Mindful living requires bringing your attention to the present moment, without judgment or distraction. As an introvert, your love for solitude and reflection can be powerful in cultivating a more mindful way of living. Start by establishing a morning routine that provides you with space and time for introspection. This could include journaling, meditation, or simply taking a quiet walk.
Setting intentions for your day can help guide you towards aligning your actions with your values. This will also help you identify what drains your energy and what uplifts you. Remember that it is okay to say no to social or work-related activities that do not align with your purpose or goals.
Mindful living is not just limited to your personal time, but can also extend into your professional life. Setting boundaries at work, such as limiting distractions or taking breaks for solitude, can help you perform better and feel more fulfilled in your career. By bringing awareness and intentionality to your daily routine, you can empower your

inner introvert and live a more purposeful and mindful life.

Navigating Change and Transitions – Strategies for Adapting to New Situations and Opportunities

Change can be daunting for anyone, especially for introverts who value stability and predictability. However, change is inevitable and can also bring exciting opportunities for personal and professional growth. In this section, we will explore strategies for navigating change and transitions, allowing introverts to adapt and thrive in new situations.

Embrace the Unknown

The fear of the unknown can be paralyzing for introverts. However, instead of dwelling on what could go wrong, try to focus on the opportunities that change can bring. Remember that change often leads to new experiences, fresh perspectives, and personal growth.

Take Small Steps

When faced with a new or intimidating situation, it's easy to feel overwhelmed. To avoid becoming immobile, try taking small steps towards your goal. Break the task or situation down into manageable pieces and take things one step at a time. This approach can help to build confidence, as well as momentum.

Develop a Support System

Change can be stressful, but having a support system in

place can help to mitigate some of the anxiety. Connect with like-minded people who can offer encouragement, advice, and support. Whether it's a trusted friend, family member, or mentor, having someone to lean on can make a world of difference.

Practice Self-Care

Navigating change and transitions can be emotionally taxing, so it's important to practice self-care. Take time to engage in activities that bring you joy and relaxation, such as meditating, yoga, or reading a favorite book. Remember to prioritize your mental and physical health during times of transition.

Monitor Your Progress

As you navigate change and adapt to new situations, it's important to monitor your progress. Celebrate small victories and take note of areas where you still need improvement. Tracking your progress can help you to stay motivated and maintain a positive mindset.

By utilizing these strategies for navigating change and transitions, introverts can embrace new situations and opportunities with confidence and purpose.

The Power of Intention – Setting Goals and Building Momentum for Continued Growth

As introverts, it can be challenging to identify our motivations and passions in a world that sometimes feels overwhelming. However, once we take the time to understand ourselves, there is no end to what we can achieve.

The key is to empower our inner introvert by setting goals and building momentum for continued growth. This all starts with the power of intention.

Intention allows us to identify our most authentic desires and what truly matters to us. It also gives us the resolve to persevere through obstacles and setbacks.

To tap into the power of intention, first, take the time to reflect on your values and what you want to achieve. Then, set clear and specific goals that align with your introspective values. This will help guide your decisions and focus your efforts towards meaningful pursuits.

Additionally, building momentum for continued growth is important in helping us achieve our goals. Break down your objectives into manageable steps and celebrate each milestone along the way. This will help to maintain motivation and build confidence in your ability to succeed.

Ultimately, by harnessing the power of intention and setting goals, we can empower ourselves to lead fulfilling lives as introverts.

Chapter 2: The Science of Introversion: Unraveling the Mysteries

The Neuroscience of Introversion

The Introvert's Brain: Understanding the Differences in Brain Chemistry

Have you ever wondered why some people are more sensitive than others or why some people need more downtime after social interactions than others? The answer may lie in their brain chemistry.

Research has shown that introverts and extroverts have different levels of activity in their prefrontal cortex – the part of the brain responsible for our ability to process information, make decisions, and control impulses. In introverts, this area tends to be more active which means they are more reflective and thoughtful in their approach to life. On the other hand, in extroverts, this area tends to be less active which makes them more outgoing, impulsive, and socially bold.

Another critical difference between an introvert and an extrovert's brain is their response to dopamine. Dopamine is a neurotransmitter that is responsible for our feelings of pleasure and reward. It's released in response to things like food, sex, and social interaction. However, the brains of introverts and extroverts respond differently to this neurotransmitter. Extroverts have more active dopamine reward pathways which make them more sensitive to rewards and more likely to seek out social interaction. Introverts, on the other hand, have less active dopamine reward pathways, which makes them less sensitive to rewards and less likely to seek out social interaction.

Understanding these differences in brain chemistry can help introverts recognize that their need for downtime and reflective thinking is a natural part of their personality, and not something that they need to change to fit in with an extroverted-dominated society. Additionally, it can help introverts appreciate their unique strengths, such as their ability to think deeply and introspectively, and use them to their advantage in various life situations.

How Neurotransmitters Affect Personality Traits

When it comes to understanding the science behind introversion, it is impossible to overlook the role of neurotransmitters. These chemicals are responsible for transmitting signals within the brain and are instrumental in shaping our personalities.

One neurotransmitter that has received significant attention within the context of introversion is dopamine. Dopamine is associated with reward-driven behavior, and researchers have found that introverts tend to have higher levels of dopamine activity in certain areas of the brain. This heightened response to reward may explain why introverts tend to prefer quieter, less stimulating environments, as they find them more rewarding than extroverts do.

On the other hand, extroverts tend to have higher levels of acetylcholine, another neurotransmitter that is associated with increased arousal and attention. This may explain why extroverts tend to thrive in social situations where there is a lot of stimulation and activity.

While these neurotransmitters may play a significant role in shaping our personalities, it is important to note that they are not the sole determining factor. Environmental and genetic factors also come into play, and the interplay between these various factors is the subject of ongoing research.

Despite the complexity of the brain, understanding the role of neurotransmitters can offer valuable insights into introversion and how it shapes our behavior and preferences. By embracing our introverted nature and recognizing the unique strengths that come with it, we can build fulfilling and successful lives both professionally and personally.

Nature vs. Nurture: The Role of Genetics in Introversion

One of the longstanding debates in the field of psychology and neuroscience is the extent to which our disposition towards introversion or extroversion is a product of genetics versus environmental factors. While both genetic and environmental factors are undoubtedly at play, recent research suggests that genetics play a significant role in shaping our personality traits.

Several studies have identified specific genes that correlate with introversion. For example, research on the COMT gene, which is involved in dopamine regulation, has found that individuals who have a certain variant are more likely to be introverted. Other studies have found that the DRD4 gene, which is involved in the regulation of dopamine receptors, may also affect introversion.

Notably, these genetic correlations do not necessarily make introversion an unchangeable trait. The same genes that predispose someone towards introversion can be expressed differently depending on environmental factors. For example, some studies have found that individuals who were highly sensitive and introverted as children were more likely to turn towards extroversion in adulthood if they grew up in a supportive and accepting environment.

In sum, while genetics undoubtedly play a role in determining our personality traits and predispositions, it is also important to remember that environmental factors can significantly shape these traits as well. By understanding the role of genetics in introversion, we can gain a better understanding of ourselves and our unique strengths and challenges.

The Importance of Environment in Shaping Introverted Traits

One of the most interesting aspects of introversion is how the environment can shape and influence introverted traits. In fact, research has shown that environmental factors can play a role in determining whether someone is more introverted or extroverted.

For example, studies have found that highly stimulating environments, such as noisy or chaotic workplaces, can be overwhelming for introverts and cause them to become depleted much faster than their extroverted counterparts. This is because introverts tend to have a more highly reactive nervous system, which means they are more sensitive to external stimuli.

On the other hand, quieter and more peaceful environments tend to be much more conducive to introverted qualities. In such environments, introverts often thrive because they are able to focus more deeply, think more creatively, and process information more thoroughly.

It's important to note that while external factors can shape an individual's introverted traits, they do not determine them entirely. Rather, it's up to each person to identify and cultivate the environments and experiences that allow them to thrive and be their best selves. Through a greater understanding of the neuroscience of introversion, introverts can take proactive steps to shape their lives in ways that support their inherent strengths and abilities.

The Connection Between Introversion and Creativity

In recent years, there has been a growing fascination with the link between introversion and creativity. Many renowned artists, writers, and musicians have been characterized as introverts, leading some experts to question whether there is truly a correlation between introversion and creative genius. While there is no clear-cut answer, it appears that there is indeed a connection between the two.

To understand this link, it's important to first examine the neuroscientific basis of introversion. Researchers have identified several brain areas that tend to be more active in introverted individuals. For example, introverts have been shown to have greater activity in the default mode network (DMN), a cluster of brain regions involved in social cognition and self-reflection. This increased activity suggests that introverts have a heightened sensitivity to their own thoughts and feelings, which may be key to their creative expression.

When it comes to creativity, there are several theories as to why introverts might excel. One possibility is that their heightened sensitivity to their own experiences allows them to engage in deep, focused reflection. This introspective process can lead to novel insights and ideas that might be more difficult to achieve through extroverted means. Additionally, introverts tend to be more prone to solitude and introspection, which can be fertile ground for creative inspiration.

There is also evidence to suggest that introverts may be more likely to engage in deliberate practice, or the focused, intentional effort to improve a specific skill. This type of practice has been shown to be a key predictor of expert level performance in various domains, including music and chess. Because introverts are less likely to become distracted by external stimuli and social interaction, they may be better suited to this type of focused practice.

While the link between introversion and creativity is still being explored, there is evidence to suggest that there is indeed a connection. Understanding the neuroscience behind introversion can help us to better appreciate the unique strengths that introverts bring to creative pursuits. Additionally, recognizing the value of solitude and introspection for generating new ideas can help introverted individuals to embrace their creative potential.

Introversion and Psychology

Carl Jung and the Theory of Introverted vs. Extroverted Personality Types

Carl Jung, the founder of analytical psychology, was one of the first psychologists to bring the concept of introversion and extroversion to mainstream attention. He believed that every individual possesses either an introverted or an extroverted personality type. Introverts, according to Jung, are people who are more focused on their own inner experiences, thoughts, and feelings, whereas extroverts are more oriented towards the external world and are energized by social interactions.

Jung's theory of introverted and extroverted personality types is based on four key factors: perception, attitude, function, and adaptation. According to Jung, introverts have a subjective perception of the world, meaning that they tend to see the world through the lens of their own inner experiences and emotions, and prioritize their own internal world. On the other hand, extroverts have an objective perception of the world, which means that they are more focused on the external world and the people and objects around them.

In terms of attitude, Jung believed that introverts have an inward-focused attitude, which makes them more thoughtful, reflective, and introspective. In contrast, extroverts have an outward-focused attitude, which makes them more action-oriented, outgoing, and assertive.

Jung's theory also highlights the difference in how

introverts and extroverts use their cognitive functions. For introverts, the dominant cognitive function is internal intuition or subjective perception, while extroverts rely more heavily on their extroverted thinking or objective judgment.

Finally, Jung believed that introverts and extroverts have different coping styles, with introverts being more likely to withdraw or retreat from social situations when they become overwhelming, while extroverts tend to seek out stimulation and engage more actively with their environment.

Although the Jungian theory of introverted and extroverted personality types has been debated and critiqued over the years, it nonetheless remains an influential framework for understanding personality and behavior. Developing an understanding of this theory can help introverts to better recognize their own tendencies and preferences and to leverage their strengths in a world that often values extroversion over introversion.

The Five Factor Model and the Trait of Introversion

The Five Factor Model (FFM) is a popular and widely-studied theory that aims to explain the five core dimensions of personality. These dimensions — commonly referred to as the "Big Five" — include openness to experience, conscientiousness, extraversion, agreeableness, and neuroticism.

Extraversion and introversion are often contrasted with

each other within the FFM, with extraversion being considered the opposite to introversion. According to the FFM, extraverts are generally more outgoing, assertive, and sociable, while introverts are typically more reserved, introspective, and thoughtful.

While the FFM is a valuable model for studying personality, some researchers have criticized its limitations in fully capturing the complexity of personality traits. For example, some argue that the FFM is limited when it comes to capturing certain traits unique to introverts, such as sensitivity to stimuli and a preference for solitude.

Despite these criticisms, the FFM remains a useful framework for considering the trait of introversion within the larger context of personality research. By using this model, we can begin to understand how different traits interact with each other to form a complete picture of our unique personalities.

The Relationship Between Introversion and Emotional Intelligence

Emotional intelligence is the ability to understand and manage emotional information, whether it be your own emotions or those of others. It is a vital component of successful interactions, particularly in the workplace. While introverted individuals have often been stereotyped as lacking in social skills, research has shown that introversion and emotional intelligence can go hand-in-hand.

One reason for this is that introverts tend to be more introspective and reflective, leading to a greater awareness of their own emotions. They may also enjoy deeper, more meaningful relationships with a smaller group of people, which can lead to a greater understanding of the nuances of social interactions. In fact, research has shown that introverts can often read others' emotions more accurately than extroverts.

However, it is important to note that not all introverts are emotionally intelligent, and not all emotionally intelligent individuals are introverted. Emotional intelligence is a skill that can be developed through practice and effort, regardless of one's introverted or extroverted tendencies.

For introverts looking to enhance their emotional intelligence, there are several strategies that can help. These include practicing active listening, seeking feedback from others, and focusing on nonverbal communication cues. Additionally, introverts may benefit from taking breaks from social interactions to reflect on their own emotions and recharge.

Ultimately, introversion and emotional intelligence are not mutually exclusive. With awareness and effort, introverted individuals are well-positioned to develop strong emotional intelligence skills and thrive in both their personal and professional lives.

Understanding Introverted Thinking vs. Extraverted Thinking

One of the key differences between introverted and extraverted individuals lies in the way they process and respond to information. While extraverts tend to rely on external stimuli and constantly seek new experiences, introverts are more likely to rely on their own internal world of thoughts and ideas. This fundamental difference in thinking styles has important implications for how introverts interact with the world around them.

Introverted thinking is characterized by a focus on internal processing and reflection. Rather than jumping into action, introverted thinkers prefer to take the time to carefully consider their options and weigh the pros and cons of different courses of action. They are often highly analytical and detail-oriented, and they place great value on accuracy and precision in their thinking.

In contrast, extraverted thinking is characterized by a more outward-focused approach. Extraverted thinkers tend to be more action-oriented and are adept at problem-solving in the moment. They often enjoy the challenge of taking on new tasks and may see their ability to think on their feet as a key strength.

While both thinking styles have their unique strengths, introverted thinking can be particularly valuable in certain contexts. For example, in highly complex or abstract fields such as science and philosophy, introverted thinking can be a powerful tool for deep analysis and exploration of complex ideas. Similarly, in creative pursuits such as writing or music composition, introverted thinking can be instrumental in developing unique and nuanced perspectives on the world.

However, introverted thinking can also present challenges in certain social situations. For example, introverted thinkers may struggle to communicate their ideas effectively to others, or may be perceived as overly critical or nitpicky. They may also be more prone to indecision or overthinking, which can hinder their ability to take action when necessary.

Thus, it is important for introverts to recognize the strengths and limitations of their thinking style and to develop strategies for communicating effectively with others. By doing so, they can harness their unique strengths as introverts while also building strong connections and thriving in the world around them.

The Benefits and Drawbacks of Introverted Sensing

The individuals who possess an introverted personality type have a cognitive preference that drives the way they connect with the world. One such preference is introverted sensing, a function that plays an essential role in shaping the introverted experience.
Introverted sensing is a cognitive function that allows individuals to take in the physical and sensory experiences of their surroundings, process them internally, and store them as memories that can be retrieved as needed. People who possess this function as their dominant or auxiliary function tend to be detail-oriented and observant, relying on concrete information and past experiences to make sense of the present.

One of the benefits of the introverted sensing function is that it enables individuals to have a rich sensory experience of the world around them. They are aware of small details and nuances that others might overlook, allowing them to find beauty in simplicity. This is particularly useful in professional contexts where precision and attention to detail are essential, such as in fields like engineering, architecture, and design.

However, it can also become a drawback in situations that require the ability to adapt to new and changing circumstances. Individuals who rely heavily on introverted sensing may struggle with activities that require them to adapt to new or novel situations, as this can disrupt their internal sensory world. They can become overwhelmed and disoriented when their patterns and routines are disrupted. This can lead to a reluctance to take risks and try new things, hindering their personal and professional growth.

Despite these potential drawbacks, the introverted sensing function can be a valuable asset when leveraged in the right context. It is important for individuals to recognize their cognitive preferences and learn how to use them effectively to achieve their goals. Those who possess strong introverted sensing skills can thrive in careers that require meticulous attention to detail, and can contribute a unique perspective to the teams they work with.

Social and Cultural Aspects of Introversion

Introverted vs. Outgoing Cultures: The Cultural Roots of Personality Differences

In this section, we'll explore how introversion and extroversion are culturally embedded and how this can contribute to the development of diverse personality traits. We'll discuss how culture shapes our beliefs, values, and behaviors, and examine how cultural factors can impact whether a person is likely to be introverted or extroverted.

We'll begin by debunking the misconception that introversion and extroversion are universal personality traits that transcend cultural boundaries. In reality, cultures vary significantly in terms of how outgoing or reserved they are, and this cultural context can influence how individuals develop their personalities.

Next, we'll explore the socialization process that shapes the formation of introversion and extroversion in different cultures. We'll analyze how cultural norms and expectations influence the ways in which introverts and extroverts are perceived and treated in different societies, and the challenges this presents for introverts.

Finally, we'll address the issue of cultural bias, which can lead to stereotypes and misunderstandings about introverts and extroverts. We'll discuss the importance of cultural sensitivity and understanding, and how to develop strategies for navigating cultural differences with confidence and self-awareness. By the end of this subsection, readers will have a deep appreciation for how cultural factors can influence personality development and have practical strategies for dealing with the different behavior patterns in introverted and outgoing cultures.

Socialization and Development of Introverted Personality Traits

Socialization and Development of Introverted Personality Traits

From childhood, socialization is a fundamental aspect of human growth, as individuals learn how to interact, communicate, and integrate into society. However, introverted individuals experience socialization differently from their extroverted counterparts. Introverted personalities tend to be introspective and thoughtful, preferring solitary or quiet activities to being in the midst of a crowd. The socialization and developmental environment of introverts have a significant impact on their personality.

Socialization is a critical determinant in the development of introverted traits. Parents, relatives, and peers play influential roles in shaping introverted behavior. Typically, introverted children find it challenging to build relationships, speak aloud in public, and express themselves openly. The socialization patterns of introverted individuals often result in feelings of isolation, loneliness, and anxiety. As children, introverts may be labeled "shy" and may experience social exclusion. This leads to further isolation and a lack of self-confidence.

However, an introverted child's quiet and reflective nature can also be a source of strength. Their introspective tendencies often lead to a more profound awareness of self, an appreciation for inner world exploration, and resilience. Parents, guardians, and educators can support introverted children by allowing them to develop at their own pace, respect their need for solitude, and encourage them to exercise their unique strengths.

Social and cultural factors also influence the development of introverted personality traits. In some cultures, a more introverted personality may be valued and even preferred over extroverted behavior. For instance, in Asian cultures, reserved and reflective individuals are often viewed as thoughtful, wise, and worthy of respect. These cultural nuances not only impact the development of introverted behavior but also shape social interactions.

In the workplace, introverted tendencies may be misunderstood or undervalued. Social norms and expectations may favor extroverted behaviors such as speaking up in meetings, participating in group activities, and engaging in small talk. However, understanding the value of introverted strengths, such as active listening, thoughtful analysis, and focused concentration, is critical in creating an inclusive and holistic work environment.

Understanding the social and cultural influences on introverted behavior helps to demystify introversion, providing insight into how an individual's personality is shaped. By acknowledging the various factors that impact the development of introverted traits, individuals can better understand their unique strengths, appreciate their personal growth journey, and foster a sense of acceptance and self-confidence.

Stereotypes and Misconceptions Surrounding Introversion

As introversion gains more attention in popular culture, so do the myths and stereotypes surrounding it. It's important to address these misconceptions head-on and educate others on the truths about introverted individuals.

One common misconception is that introverts are antisocial or standoffish. This is far from the truth - introverts simply prefer deeper, more meaningful connections and may not enjoy small talk and superficial interactions as much as extroverts do. In fact, many introverts are highly empathetic and make great listeners and supportive friends.

Another stereotype is that introverts are always quiet and reserved. While this may be true in some situations, introverts can be outgoing and engaging when they are passionate about a topic or with people they are comfortable with. Furthermore, introverts often prefer to process their thoughts internally before speaking, which can sometimes make them appear less chatty than extroverts.

One particularly damaging misconception is that introverts are not leaders. This couldn't be further from the truth - introverted leaders tend to excel in areas such as listening, problem-solving, and strategic thinking. They often foster strong, loyal relationships with their team members and lead with a calm, focused demeanor.

It's important to recognize that introversion is not a negative trait, and that introverts can be just as successful and valuable in social and professional settings as extroverts. By debunking these stereotypes and misconceptions, we can create a more inclusive and understanding world for everyone, regardless of their introverted or extroverted nature.

The Realities of Being an Introvert in Modern Society

In modern society, extroversion is often viewed as the norm, and introversion is seen as a deviation from the social norm. There are countless examples of this in everyday life, from the expectation that individuals should participate in social events outside of work to the emphasis placed on group work in educational and professional settings. As a result, introverts may often feel out of place or overlooked.

In addition, social media and technology have made it easier for individuals to connect with each other, but these tools can also exacerbate the pressures faced by introverts. Social media platforms demand constant engagement and sharing, which may create anxiety for introverts who prefer to communicate on a more individual basis. At the same time, technology has enabled individuals to work remotely, which may be a desirable prospect for introverts seeking to limit their interactions with others.

Ultimately, the challenges associated with being an introvert in modern society can be difficult to navigate. However, recognizing and embracing one's introverted nature can lead to a greater sense of self-acceptance and empowerment. Additionally, there are numerous strategies and techniques that can help introverts thrive in social and professional settings, from finding ways to recharge in solitude to utilizing virtual communication tools to build connections with others. By understanding the realities of being an introvert in modern society and adopting strategies that work for them, introverts can lead fulfilling and successful lives.

How Society Can Embrace and Support the Introverted Population

Introverts have always been at a disadvantage in a society that values outgoing, gregarious behavior. However, there is a growing understanding of the importance of introverts in modern times, and efforts are being made to accommodate them. In this section, we will discuss how society can embrace and support introverts.

A. Encouraging Diversity in the Workplace

It is crucial to encourage diversity in the workplace, including introverts. Employers should embrace the fact that introverts work differently, and it is important to make changes to accommodate them. This can include flexible working hours, remote work options, and quiet spaces where they can work without distraction. By accommodating introverted employees, businesses can benefit from the unique strengths that introverts bring to the table.

B. Providing Quiet Spaces in Public Areas

Public areas need to have quiet spaces where introverts can retreat when they feel overwhelmed. This can include libraries, parks, and cafes that offer secluded areas where people can be alone with their thoughts. By creating these spaces, introverts can participate in public life without feeling drained or overwhelmed.

C. Rethinking Social Norms and Practices

Many social norms and practices, such as small talk and networking events, can be a nightmare for introverts. By rethinking these norms and practices, society can accommodate introverts and make them feel more comfortable. This can involve providing alternatives to traditional networking events, such as online forums or virtual meetups. Similarly, social interactions can be more enjoyable when they revolve around shared interests, rather than forced small talk.

D. Educating People on Introversion

Finally, society needs to be educated about the nature of introversion. Many people misunderstand what introversion is and may mistake it for shyness or social anxiety. By educating people about introversion and how to accommodate it, society can create a more supportive environment for introverts.

Conclusion:

By embracing and supporting the introverted population, society as a whole can benefit from their unique strengths and insights. By providing quiet spaces, rethinking social norms, and educating the public on introversion, we can create a more inclusive and supportive society for everyone.

Chapter 3: Myth-Busting: Debunking Introvert Stereotypes and Misconceptions

Misconceptions About Introversion

Introverts are shy and lack social skills

When people think of introverts, they often picture individuals who are shy, socially awkward, and uncomfortable in social situations. While some introverts may fit that description, it is important to understand that shyness and lack of social skills are not synonymous with introversion.

Introverts are simply individuals who prefer quieter, more contemplative environments and may find too much stimulation exhausting. They may prefer one-on-one conversations or smaller, more intimate gatherings rather than loud parties or large social events.

It is also important to note that introverts are not always shy or lacking in social skills. While they may not be as talkative or outgoing as their extroverted counterparts, introverts are capable of having meaningful conversations and building strong relationships. In fact, many introverts are excellent listeners and can pick up on subtle cues and nuances in social interactions that extroverts may miss.

It is also important to understand that shyness is not a personality trait reserved only for introverts. Shyness is a behavior that can be exhibited by both introverts and extroverts, and it is not an inherent characteristic of introversion.

By debunking the myth that introverts are shy and lack social skills, we can begin to appreciate the unique strengths and perspectives that introverts can bring to social situations, as well as the importance of creating a diverse and inclusive environment that includes both introverts and extroverts.

Introverts are not assertive or confident

Introverts are often wrongly perceived as individuals who lack assertiveness and confidence. This stereotype is further propagated by a society that values extroverted qualities such as gregariousness, boldness, and outspokenness. However, introversion and assertiveness are not mutually exclusive. Introverts can be assertive and confident without losing their inherent traits.

Assertiveness is not about being aggressive, pushy, or overbearing. Rather, it is the ability to communicate effectively and assert one's needs and desires in a respectful manner. Introverts often take the time to reflect and prepare their thoughts before speaking up, which can come across as hesitancy or a lack of confidence. However, this is simply a result of their thought process and should not be misinterpreted as a lack of assertiveness.

Introverts can excel in assertiveness by using their natural strengths, such as careful listening, deep thinking, and insightful observations, to make well-informed decisions and effectively communicate their opinions. By doing so, they can add value to their team or organization and make a positive impact on those they interact with.

Confidence is another trait that introverts are often unfairly stereotyped as lacking. However, like assertiveness, confidence is not a one-dimensional characteristic. Introverts can be confident in their abilities and ideas, despite not outwardly displaying it through loud or bold behavior.

To cultivate confidence, introverts can focus on their strengths, set achievable goals, and celebrate their successes, no matter how small they may seem. By learning to accept and embrace their introverted nature, they can develop a sense of self-worth and belief in themselves that will radiate outwardly, positively impacting their career and personal life.

Introverts are often unfairly stereotyped as lacking assertiveness and confidence. However, introversion and these qualities are not mutually exclusive. By using their natural strengths and embracing their introverted nature, introverts can be both assertive and confident, making a positive impact on their career and personal life.

Introverts are not creative or innovative

Introverts have long been viewed as the antithesis of creativity and innovation. The stereotype suggests that because they tend to be more reserved and quieter, they lack the boldness and confidence required to generate new ideas or make daring moves. However, studies have shown that this couldn't be further from the truth.

For example, research has shown that introverts tend to approach problems in a more focused, thorough manner than extroverts. This conscientiousness, paired with strong analytical thinking skills, can lead to more innovative thinking over time. In one study, participants were asked to brainstorm new business ideas. The introverts in the group generated significantly more good ideas than extroverts, despite the fact that they spoke less often overall.

Furthermore, introverts also tend to excel in creative fields where they can work independently. Studies have shown that introverted artists, writers, and musicians often produce work that is just as creative and innovative as their extroverted peers. For example, J.K. Rowling, the author of the hugely successful Harry Potter series, has described herself as a "quite innovative introvert."

Ultimately, the belief that introverts are not creative or innovative is a harmful one that needs to be challenged. By recognizing and valuing introverted strengths, we can create environments that encourage all types of thinkers to thrive and succeed.

Introverts are not effective leaders

There is a common misconception that introverts do not make effective leaders. This belief is rooted in the misconception that a good leader needs to be outgoing, assertive, and charismatic. While those are certainly desirable traits, they are by no means the only ones that make a successful leader.

In fact, research has shown that introverts can be incredibly effective leaders. Introverted leaders are often thoughtful, analytical, and empathetic. They take the time to listen to others and consider different perspectives before making decisions. They are also less likely to be swayed by the opinions of others and more likely to stay true to their own convictions.

However, it is true that introverted leaders can face unique challenges in certain situations. For example, they may struggle with public speaking or networking, which are often seen as essential skills for a leader. They may also be perceived as being aloof or unapproachable, which can make it difficult to build strong relationships with team members.

Despite these challenges, introverted leaders can still be incredibly effective if they learn to play to their strengths and develop strategies for overcoming their weaknesses. For example, introverted leaders can focus on building strong one-on-one relationships with team members rather than relying on networking events. They can also prepare thoroughly for public speaking engagements and make an effort to project warmth and approachability.

Ultimately, the key to being an effective leader is not in being an extrovert or an introvert, but in understanding your own strengths and weaknesses and learning to adapt to different situations. Introverts can be just as successful as extroverts if they are willing to embrace their unique qualities and use them to their advantage.

Introverts are not team players

Introverts are often perceived to be aloof and not willing to work with others. This couldn't be further from the truth. While introverts tend to prefer solo work or small group interactions, they are often great team players. In fact, some studies have shown that teams with a mix of introverts and extroverts tend to perform better than homogeneous teams.

The misconception that introverts are not team players comes from the assumption that being a good team player means being outgoing, talkative, and charismatic. However, these traits do not necessarily equate to teamwork. Effective teamwork requires communication, collaboration, and understanding of each other's strengths and weaknesses.

Introverts can be great team players because they tend to be good listeners, thoughtful contributors, and can offer unique perspectives. They also prefer to work in smaller groups, which can lead to better discussions and more efficient decision-making processes.

It's important to note that introverts may need more time to process their thoughts before contributing to a group discussion. This should not be mistaken for detachment or apathy towards the team's goals. Instead, it is a natural behavior that can be managed with understanding and patience from the team.

The misconception that introverts are not team players is unfounded. With their unique strengths and abilities, introverts can make valuable contributions to any team environment. It's important to recognize and embrace these differences to foster a productive and inclusive work culture for all personality types.

Common Myths About Extroversion

Extroverts are always outgoing and confident

It's easy to assume that all extroverts are outgoing and confident, but this is not always the case. In reality, extroversion is not a one-size-fits-all personality trait. While some extroverts may have outgoing personalities, others may be more reserved and introspective.

For instance, a party-loving extrovert may come across as hyper and on-the-go, but another extrovert might be comfortable in a crowd but still quiet and not the center of attention. Confidence is also not a defining trait of extroverts. Just like introverts, extroverts could struggle with self-doubt and low self-esteem. Some extroverts might even use their social connections as a way to mask their insecurities.

In fact, studies show that extroverts can feel drained and overstimulated by too much social interaction, just like introverts. They may require quiet time to recharge and reflect upon the events of the day.

The important thing to remember is that extroversion is not a one-dimensional trait. Just as there is more to introversion than simply being shy and quiet, there is more to extroversion than just being outgoing and confident. We all possess nuances that can't be defined by a label, and it's these differences that make us unique.

Extroverts are better communicators than introverts

In this section, we'll explore the common myths about extroverts and shed light on the misconceptions that tend to surround them. As we delve into the world of extroversion, we'll examine how certain beliefs about extroverts being better communicators than their introverted counterparts don't necessarily hold up under closer inspection.

It's true that extroverts tend to have an easier time striking up conversations with others and may appear more socially confident. However, this does not necessarily mean that they are innately better communicators. In fact, some studies suggest that introverts may have distinct advantages when it comes to communication.

For instance, introverts often take time to carefully consider their words before speaking, which can make their messages more thoughtful and impactful. They may also be better at active listening, as they tend to focus more on the speaker and their message rather than on their own thoughts and ideas.

Additionally, introverts may be better at adapting their communication style to different situations or individuals. They may effectively use active listening, open-ended questions, and empathy to build rapport with others and facilitate meaningful conversations.

In reality, communication skills are not necessarily determined by one's personality type, but rather are developed through deliberate practice and effort. By understanding and working with our unique strengths as introverts or extroverts, we can hone our communication skills and excel in social and professional settings.

Extroverts are better leaders than introverts

In this section, we will debunk the myth that extroverts are better leaders than introverts. While it may seem like extroverts have a natural advantage in leadership due to their outgoing nature, research suggests otherwise.

Firstly, let's understand what makes a great leader. Contrary to popular belief, it's not about being extroverted or outgoing. Leadership is about inspiring and motivating others, setting a vision and working towards it, and making tough decisions when necessary. Introverts can possess all of these qualities just as easily as extroverts.

In fact, some of the most successful and admired leaders in history have been introverts. Take Mahatma Gandhi, for example, who led India to independence through his quiet strength and determination. Or Rosa Parks, who sparked the civil rights movement simply by refusing to give up her seat on a bus. These are both introverts who changed the world through their leadership abilities.

Research also supports the idea that introverts can be just as effective leaders as extroverts. A study by Harvard Business Review found that quiet and introverted leaders can be more effective than their loud and extroverted counterparts in certain situations, such as when leading proactive teams who don't need constant supervision.

Furthermore, introverts bring a unique set of skills and strengths to the table that can benefit their leadership abilities. These include active listening, thoughtful decision-making, and a tendency to form deep and meaningful relationships with team members.

It's important to remember that leadership is not a one-size-fits-all approach. Both introverts and extroverts can be exceptional leaders, and there is no one right way to lead. By recognizing and embracing our differences, we can create more inclusive and effective leadership teams that benefit everyone involved.

Extroverts don't need alone time or quiet environments

It's a common misconception that extroverts thrive in socializing and can't stand spending time alone or in quiet environments. However, that's not entirely true. While extroverts do enjoy being around people, they also need alone time to recharge their batteries and reflect on their thoughts.

Extroverts can also appreciate the value of a quiet environment in certain situations. For example, if they're trying to focus on a task or engage in deep conversation, they may prefer a quieter setting to avoid distractions.

It's important to note that extroversion and introversion exist on a spectrum, and individuals may have varying levels of each trait. Therefore, it's not accurate to make sweeping generalizations about a person's preferences based solely on their personality type.

By understanding and debunking these myths about extroverts, introverts can learn to appreciate and engage with extroverted individuals in a more effective and respectful manner.

Extroverts are always energized by social interactions

One common myth about extroverts is that they are always energized by social interactions. While it's true that many extroverts do gain energy from being around people, it's important to recognize that this isn't always the case.

Just like introverts, extroverts are individuals with their own unique needs and preferences. Some may feel invigorated by big groups and lively conversations, while others may find these situations overwhelming or draining.

It's also worth noting that social interactions aren't the only way that extroverts can gain energy. Some may find that they feel most alive when engaging in physical activities, exploring new places, or pursuing their passions.

Ultimately, it's important to recognize that being an extrovert doesn't necessarily mean that you are always the life of the party. Just like introverts, extroverts have their own strengths and challenges, and it's up to each individual to honor their own needs and preferences.

Debunking Stereotypes and Embracing Differences

Embracing and celebrating introversion instead of trying to change

In this subsection, we will explore the advantages of embracing and celebrating introversion instead of trying to change it. Society often values extroverted qualities such as sociability, assertiveness, and gregariousness over introverted traits like introspection, thoughtfulness, and reflection. Introverts are often made to feel inadequate or wrong for being quiet or reserved, which can lead to feelings of shame and inadequacy.

However, recent research shows that introverts have distinct strengths that can be leveraged for personal and professional success. Introverts are often more focused, reflective, and analytical than their extroverted counterparts. They also tend to have a greater capacity for empathy and deeper connections with others. By embracing these unique qualities, introverts can finally reject the stigma that society attaches to their nature and instead celebrate their strengths.

This begins with a shift of focus from changing oneself to accepting and celebrating oneself. It means learning to recognize and honor your own unique voice and values, as well as valuing the insights and contributions that only introverts can bring. Whether it means setting aside quiet time to recharge or expressing oneself through a medium like writing or art, there are many avenues for introverts to cultivate their strengths and flourish in a world that can't stop talking.

Understanding the unique qualities introverts bring to the table

In this section, we will explore the unique qualities that introverts bring to the table. They may not be as readily apparent as extroverted qualities, but they are no less valuable or impactful. For starters, introverts are often great listeners due to their innate ability to focus deeply on a topic or conversation. By tuning out distractions and honing in on the speaker, introverts can pick up on nuances and read between the lines.

Moreover, while introverts may not be the most outwardly expressive people, they are often very reflective and introspective. This can lead to deep insights and creative solutions to problems that may not have been considered by others. Introverts have a rich inner world, and their introspection allows them to tap into this world and bring new ideas to the table.

An introvert's calm, measured approach to situations can also be a valuable asset. While extroverts may be more likely to jump into action, introverts are known for weighing their options and considering all the angles before making a move. This can be particularly helpful in high-pressure situations where making the wrong decision can have serious consequences.

Lastly, introverts are typically self-sufficient and don't require constant stimulation or attention from others. This independence can lead to a strong work ethic and a willingness to tackle tasks alone when necessary. The ability to work independently can be a great asset in business and can set introverts apart from their extroverted peers.

By understanding and embracing these unique qualities, introverts can confidently navigate social and professional situations, knowing that their skills are just as valuable as those of their extroverted counterparts.

Benefits of introvert-extrovert collaboration and communication

In a world that often favors extroversion, introverts can sometimes feel left out or undervalued. However, when introverts and extroverts work together, their differences can lead to positive outcomes and enhance team performance.

While introverts tend to work well independently and in quieter environments, extroverts thrive in group settings and enjoy brainstorming and bouncing ideas off others. When these two personality types collaborate, introverts can offer insightful analysis and critical thinking, while extroverts can bring energy and enthusiasm to the group.

Furthermore, introverts can help extroverts slow down and think more deeply about their ideas, while extroverts can encourage introverts to speak up and share their insights. By embracing each other's differences and leveraging their strengths, introvert-extrovert teams can achieve great success.

Effective communication is also crucial in introvert-extrovert collaboration. Introverts may prefer written communication, while extroverts may thrive in verbal discussions. By finding a balance between these communication styles, team members can ensure everyone is heard and their ideas are integrated into the group's work.

Introvert-extrovert collaboration can lead to diverse perspectives, increased creativity, and successful outcomes. By embracing differences and leveraging each other's strengths, introverts and extroverts can work together effectively and thrive in a variety of settings.

The dangers of sterotyping people based on their personality types

Introduction:
In this section, we will discuss how introverts have long been misunderstood and how their unique qualities have been perceived as flaws. We will explore the innate differences between introverts and extroverts and the strengths that introverts bring to the table. In this particular subsection, we focus on the dangers of stereotyping people based on their personality types.

Body:
Stereotyping people based on their personality types can be dangerous, limiting, and harmful. For introverts, they may feel unaccepted or wrongly judged for the way they interact and communicate with others. Moreover, stereotyping can lead to exclusion in the workplace, social events or groups, and any other areas where interaction with others is necessary.

Stereotyping can also lead to a lack of diversity in certain environments which can be detrimental to progress, productivity and success. When groups and organization limit diversity, often they are also limiting innovation, insight, and creativity. Therefore, recognizing and accepting differences can open doors for greater diversity of thought and collaboration.

Lastly, embracing differences can foster greater respect and empathy and widen people's minds to different perspectives. It is crucial to understand and appreciate that each person is unique and brings something unique to the table. Stereotyping does not only hurt individuals, but it can also limit the growth and morality of society as a whole.

Conclusion:
In this subsection, we highlighted the dangers of stereotyping and how it can stifle individual growth and limit diversity. It is essential to accept and celebrate differences so that people can work better together, foster more openness and respect, and promote collaboration, innovation, and a better world for everyone.

The importance of respecting boundaries and preferences of introverts and extroverts alike

In order to truly embrace introversion and debunk stereotypes, it's important to recognize and respect the boundaries and preferences of both introverts and extroverts. While it's common for extroverts to thrive in large social settings, introverts often prefer smaller gatherings or one-on-one interactions. This doesn't mean that introverts don't enjoy socializing or that extroverts don't enjoy alone time, but rather that their needs and preferences may differ.

It's important to consider these differences when planning events or social outings. For example, an introvert may feel overwhelmed and drained by a large, noisy party, while an extrovert may feel bored and unfulfilled by a small, quiet gathering. By recognizing and catering to these differences, everyone can have a better experience.

Similarly, it's important to respect individual communication styles. Introverts may be more reflective and selective in their speech, while extroverts may be more outgoing and expressive. This doesn't mean that one style is better than the other, but rather that individuals should be allowed to communicate in a way that feels natural to them.

By embracing and respecting these differences, we can create a more inclusive and understanding world for both introverts and extroverts. Both personalities have unique strengths and contributions to make, and by working together, we can achieve great things.

Chapter 4: Quiet Power: Identifying and Leveraging Your Unique Introverted Strengths

Understanding Your Introverted Personality Traits

The Power of Reflection: Understanding Yourself on a Deeper Level

As an introverted individual, it is important to realize that your personality traits are not defects, but rather valuable strengths that make you unique. Introverts are known for being deep thinkers and reflective individuals. They often possess a rich inner world that allows them to contemplate and process their experiences and emotions on a profound level.

In this subsection, we will explore the power of reflection and how it can help you develop a deeper understanding of yourself as an introvert. Reflection involves taking the time to pause and examine your thoughts, feelings, and behaviors. By doing so, you can gain insight into your underlying motivations, preferences, and needs.

To begin the process of reflection, find a quiet, comfortable space where you can be alone with your thoughts. It may also be helpful to have a journal or notebook on hand where you can jot down your observations and insights.

Start by taking several deep breaths and centering yourself in the present moment.

With a calm and focused mindset, begin to reflect on your experiences as an introverted person. What are some of the traits and characteristics that define you as an introvert? How do these traits manifest in your everyday life? Are there certain environments or situations that drain your energy or make you feel particularly uncomfortable?

Take note of any patterns or recurring themes in your reflections. Perhaps you find that you need more alone time than most people or that you are particularly sensitive to loud or chaotic surroundings. These insights can help you understand your introverted tendencies and develop strategies to manage your energy levels.

By reflecting on your introverted personality traits, you can gain a deeper understanding of yourself and appreciate the strengths that come with being an introvert. Quiet reflection can be a powerful tool for personal growth and self-awareness.

Embracing Your Need for Solitude: Recognizing the Benefits

As an introvert, you tend to experience the world in a different way than your extroverted counterparts. One of the defining characteristics of introversion is a need for solitude, which is often misunderstood and perceived as antisocial behavior. However, embracing your need for solitude can have many benefits and enable you to thrive in your personal and professional life. Here's why.

Increased Creativity: Solitude allows you to tap into your imagination and explore your thoughts and ideas without external distractions. By having time to reflect, you can come up with new and innovative ideas that you might not have otherwise.

Improved Focus: When you have solitude, you have the opportunity to concentrate on what matters the most. You can allocate time to stop multitasking and instead concentrate on one thing at a time. Interruptions, messages, and notifications decrease productivity by more than 40%, disrupting the flow of work and creating a sense of work overload. Solitude helps counteract this.

Enhanced Self-Awareness: Spending time alone enables you to become more self-aware, enhancing your understanding of your own emotions, thoughts, and behaviors. It allows you to reflect on your experiences and make necessary changes that align with your core values.

Recharged Energy: Introverts utilize solitude to recharge their batteries. In social scenarios, they expend more energy than extroverts when it comes to socializing, which is why they need time to be by themselves to recharge their energy levels so they can give their best performance in social events.

By embracing your need for solitude, you can harness your strengths as an introvert and use them to your advantage, both personally and professionally.

Leaning into Your Inner World: Cultivating a Rich Inner Life

Introverts are known for their rich inner world, full of thoughts, emotions, and ideas. They often prefer spending time alone to recharge, and they can be very introspective. This can be a strength for introverts, but it can also be a source of confusion and even anxiety. In this subsection, we will explore how introverts can cultivate a rich inner life and use it to their advantage.

Embracing solitude: For many introverts, being alone is essential for their well-being. Solitude can be a source of creativity, introspection, and self-discovery. However, solitude can also be challenging, especially in a world that values extroverted qualities. We will explore why solitude is important for introverts and how they can create spaces for solitude in their lives.

Practicing mindfulness: Mindfulness is a powerful tool for introverts to cultivate a rich inner life. By paying attention to their thoughts and emotions, introverts can better understand themselves and their motivations. We will explore how introverts can practice mindfulness and use it to their advantage.

Exploring creativity: Many introverts are naturally creative and have a unique perspective on the world. By exploring creative pursuits, introverts can express themselves and share their unique voice with the world. We will explore how introverts can tap into their creativity and use it to their advantage.

Developing self-awareness: Self-awareness is essential for introverts to navigate the world around them. By understanding their strengths, weaknesses, and motivations, introverts can make better decisions and live a more fulfilling life. We will explore how introverts can develop self-awareness and use it to their advantage.

In this subsection, we have explored how introverts can cultivate a rich inner life and use it to their advantage. By embracing solitude, practicing mindfulness, exploring creativity, and developing self-awareness, introverts can become more confident, resilient, and self-accepting.

Respecting Your Limits: Honoring Yourself and Your Energy

As an introvert, you have your unique traits that set you apart from the extroverted crowd. Understanding your introverted personality traits helps you appreciate your nature and work with the strengths you possess. However, it's essential to set healthy boundaries and respect your limits.

Introverts tend to feel drained and burned out when they are overstimulated or forced to socialize for extended periods. While it's admirable to step out of your comfort zone, you must also recognize when you've reached your limit. Respecting your limits involves learning how to say no politely and declining certain invitations or opportunities that don't serve your best interests.

Although introverts enjoy solitude, social interaction is still necessary for growth and development. However, you must find a balance between socializing and taking time for yourself. Respecting your limits means scheduling recovery periods after social events or work events that require extended periods of communication and interaction.

Your introverted nature is a valuable asset that makes you a unique and thoughtful individual. However, it's vital to respect your limits and honor your energy levels to avoid burnout and exhaustion. By setting healthy boundaries, you can excel and lead a fulfilling life, both personally and professionally.

Practicing Self-Care: Nurturing Yourself in a Busy World

As an introvert, it is essential to recognize the necessity of self-care. While extroverts may get energized by social interactions or stimulation, introverts may find themselves exhausted, therefore requiring ample time to recharge their battery. Unfortunately, our society often considers busyness as a measure of productivity, neglecting the significance of self-care.

Self-care involves prioritizing your physical, emotional, and mental health. Unlike extroverts who may feed off social interactions and external stimulation, introverts may require ample time to quiet their minds and reflect on their thoughts. Taking care of yourself may involve carving out time to practice mindfulness through meditation, journaling, or enjoying solitude. It may also include setting healthy boundaries around your social interactions, giving yourself ample time to rest and recharge.

As an introvert, it's easy to fall into the trap of self-criticism, feeling like you need to adapt to an extroverted world to excel. However, it's critical to remind yourself of your unique strengths and how they can be beneficial in navigating your personal and professional life. Practicing self-care is an essential tool to utilize your introversion to its fullest potential, helping you tap into your abilities and thrive in today's society.

The Gentle Art of Listening: The Introvert's Superpower

The Power of Active Listening: How to Connect with Others Deeply

As an introvert, you might feel that you don't have much to contribute to a conversation or that you struggle to connect with others. However, the truth is that introverts often possess exceptional listening skills, which can help them build genuine and profound connections with others.

One of the most crucial aspects of effective listening is active listening. Active listening involves fully engaging with the other person and giving them your full attention so that you can understand their perspective and respond thoughtfully. Active listening requires more than just hearing what someone is saying; it involves paying close attention to their body language, tone of voice, and underlying emotions to gain a deeper understanding of their message.

To become an active listener, start by removing any distractions and fully engaging with the other person. This means putting away your phone, closing your laptop, and making eye contact. Try to avoid interrupting them, and instead wait for them to finish speaking before responding. Additionally, ask clarifying questions to ensure that you understand their perspective fully.

When you practice active listening, you'll find that you build more profound connections with the people around you. You'll also be able to respond more thoughtfully and effectively when you engage in conversations, which can help you excel both personally and professionally. By embracing your introverted listening skills, you'll be able to communicate confidently and build stronger relationships with those around you.

The Art of Empathic Listening: Understanding and Supporting Others

Intro:

As introverts, we have the exceptional ability to listen to others without jumping in with our own thoughts and opinions. However, for many introverts, listening can be a passive activity that does not necessarily help in building meaningful relationships. In this subsection, we will explore empathic listening, a form of active listening that goes beyond hearing words and instead focuses on understanding others on a deeper level.

What is Empathic Listening?

Empathic listening is a communication technique that allows the listener to understand and respond to the speaker's feelings, beliefs, and perspective. When we engage in empathic listening, we don't just listen to the words being expressed, but also try to understand the underlying emotions and motivations behind them.

Why is Empathic Listening Important for Introverts?

Empathic listening can be particularly helpful for introverts as it offers an opportunity to build deeper connections with others without feeling the need to constantly speak or engage in small talk. Listening with empathy can also help introverts in situations where they may feel anxious or uncomfortable, as it shifts the focus away from themselves and onto the other person.

The Steps of Empathic Listening

Pay attention: Focus on the person speaking, and give them your undivided attention. Try to avoid distractions, such as checking your phone or looking around the room.

Show interest: Use body language and nonverbal cues, such as nodding your head, to show that you are interested in what the person is saying.

Paraphrase: Summarize what the person has said to demonstrate your understanding. Paraphrasing can also help the speaker clarify their own thoughts and feelings.

Reflect: Reflect the speaker's feelings back to them, using phrases such as 'I can imagine that must have been difficult for you,' or 'It sounds like you felt really frustrated.' This demonstrates that you are not only listening to their words but also trying to understand their emotions.

Ask questions: Ask open-ended questions to gain a deeper understanding of the speaker's perspective. Avoid questions that can be answered with a simple 'yes' or 'no.'

Conclusion:

Empathic listening is a powerful tool that can help introverts build deeper connections with others while also honing their own listening skills. By developing the ability to listen with empathy and understanding, introverts can contribute actively to personal and professional relationships and experience a greater sense of fulfillment and satisfaction in their interactions with others.

The Power of Silence: How to Communicate Effectively without Words

Introverts may not be known for being the most talkative people in the room, but that doesn't mean they can't communicate effectively. In fact, introverts have a powerful tool at their disposal: the power of silence.

Silence can be uncomfortable for some, but for introverts, it can be a welcome relief. Instead of feeling pressure to fill every conversational gap with words, introverts can lean into the power of silence and use it to their advantage.

One way introverts can leverage the power of silence is through active listening. By truly listening to what someone else is saying, without interrupting or formulating a response, introverts can gain a deeper understanding of the other person and their perspective.

Silence can also be a powerful tool for introverts in group settings. Rather than feeling like they need to speak up in order to contribute, introverts can quietly observe and process the conversation, ultimately offering insights and ideas that may have been overlooked by others.

But communicating effectively through silence requires intentionality. Introverts must learn to embrace moments of silence and resist the urge to fill them with unnecessary words. By doing so, they can tap into the power of silence and communicate more effectively than ever before.

Listening as a Gateway to Leadership: How to Influence Others through Listening

Listening is often seen as a passive activity, but for introverts, it can be a powerful tool for influence and leadership. By actively listening to others, introverts can build rapport, gain understanding, and inspire change.

Firstly, active listening is crucial for building rapport with others. When you listen to someone, truly listening, you convey that you value them and what they have to say. This can go a long way in building relationships and trust, which are essential in any kind of leadership role.

Once you have built a rapport and established trust, listening can also help you gain a deeper understanding of those you lead. By truly listening to their perspectives, concerns, and ideas, you can gain a more comprehensive view of the situation at hand. This allows you to make more informed decisions and ultimately lead more effectively.

Finally, active listening can be a powerful tool for inspiring change. By listening to others and understanding their perspectives, you can identify common ground and potential solutions. This can help you to engage others in shared goals and create a sense of collective purpose.

Listening is far from a passive activity – it can be a powerful tool for influence and leadership. By actively listening to others, introverts can build rapport, gain understanding, and inspire change in the organizations and communities they serve.

Cultivating Your Listening Skills: Practical Strategies for Listening Mastery

As introverts, we all have our unique set of strengths we can leverage to thrive in a world that often favors the extroverted. One of the most valuable abilities we possess is our talent for listening.

Listening is a crucial communication skill that has immense benefits in social, personal, and professional settings. For introverts, it's a superpower that allows us to connect with people, understand their needs, and respond thoughtfully with empathy and authenticity.

Yet, listening is often overlooked or undervalued in a world that values speaking, acting, and being assertive. Many of us struggle to listen, either due to a lack of interest or a tendency to get distracted or tune out. However, cultivating our listening skills is vital, and it's possible to develop them through practical strategies and techniques.

In this section, we will explore some of the most effective strategies you can use to cultivate your listening skills and master the art of active listening. These techniques can help you develop a deeper, more meaningful understanding of the people you interact with and build stronger relationships with them.

One of the essential aspects of effective listening is paying attention. While this may sound easy, staying attentive to what someone is saying requires concentration, focus, and mental effort. Distractions such as your thoughts, environmental factors, or other stimuli can quickly derail your attention.

To improve your listening skills, you need to develop mindfulness— the practice of being fully present and centered in the moment. Mindfulness helps you stay attuned to your surroundings, emotions, and physical sensations, and be more responsive to others.

Another critical skill to master is questioning. Asking probing questions is a powerful tool to gain new insights, uncover hidden information, and encourage others to open up. Open-ended questions that start with words like how, why, or what, are more effective than yes/no questions because they prompt people to think more critically and share more elaborated responses.

Finally, it's crucial to develop your empathic listening skills. Empathy is the ability to understand, share, and connect with someone else's feelings and experiences. It's a powerful, relationship-building quality that can help you build rapport, trust, and respect with others.

To cultivate empathic listening, focus on being more sensitive to others' emotions and body language. Try to put yourself in their shoes and imagine how they're feeling. Validate their emotions by acknowledging their point of view, and respond in a supportive, non-judgmental way.

With these techniques, you can become a more effective listener and unlock the full potential of your introverted superpower. By cultivating your listening skills, you can build stronger relationships, become a better collaborator, and inspire trust, respect, and influence.

Harnessing the Power of Focus: The Introvert's Secret Weapon

Understanding the Introvert's Unique Ability to Focus

As an introvert, you possess a remarkable ability to focus intently on tasks and ideas that interest you. This intense focus allows you to dive deeply into subject matter, giving you a level of expertise that is difficult for extroverts to match.

To understand why introverts are so adept at focus, it's important to explore the science behind our cognitive processes. Introverts have been found to have lower levels of arousal in their brains than extroverts, which means they require less external stimulation to feel alert and focused. This can be a double-edged sword, as it also means introverts can become overstimulated easily.

Due to their heightened sensitivity to their environment, introverts are often more selective about what they focus on. They may be less interested in socializing or networking, for example, and instead, channel their energies into deep projects, work, or hobbies. This contemplative nature can help to fuel their intense focus, enabling them to learn and create at higher levels than more extroverted counterparts.

Furthermore, introverts tend to enjoy working independently, which empowers their focus even further. This preference for solitude enhances their natural ability to block out distractions and allows them to enter a flow state in which they can work for hours without interruption.

In order to leverage their unique ability to focus, introverts need to first identify the types of tasks and environments that they find most conducive to concentration. Once this awareness is established, they can set up their workspaces and schedules to maximize their focus and productivity.

By understanding and honing their innate ability to focus, introverts can unlock a tremendous source of power and creativity that can propel them towards greater success in their personal and professional lives.

Tapping into Deep Work: How to Use Focus to Achieve Mastery

As an introvert, focusing deeply on a project or task can be one of your greatest strengths. This ability to block out distractions and devote your full self to a single endeavor is a skill that can lead to mastery and success.

To tap into this power of focus, it's essential first to understand what deep work means. Essentially, deep work is the state of being wholly concentrated and free from distractions or interruptions. It involves moving beyond the surface level and into a state of flow, where time seems to slip away, and you're wholly engrossed in the task at hand.

One essential key to achieving deep work is setting boundaries. As an introvert, you're likely already familiar with the importance of creating a quiet, private space where you can retreat from the world. Similarly, creating clear boundaries around your time and energy is necessary to allow you to focus without distraction. This could mean turning off your phone, setting specific work hours, or communicating your needs to family members or coworkers.

Another critical aspect of tapping into deep work is building the habit of sustained focus. Like most skills, focus takes practice and discipline to develop. By gradually increasing the amount of time you spend in deep work and minimizing distractions, you can train your brain to become more focused, attentive, and productive.

Finally, it's essential to recognize that while deep work can be incredibly effective, it's not a sustainable state for long periods. Just as athletes need rest and recovery after intense training, your brain needs time to recharge after concentrated periods of work. Be sure to incorporate breaks and downtime into your schedule to avoid burnout and maintain a healthy balance.

Overcoming Distractions: Practical Strategies for Maintaining Focus

As an introvert, you probably possess an incredible ability to focus deeply on your work or other interests. However, if you are like most people, you have likely experienced moments when distractions get in the way of your productivity. Whether it's the constant pinging of notifications on your phone or the chatter of coworkers, distractions can be a significant obstacle to maintaining focus.

So, how can you manage distractions effectively and stay focused on your work or goals? Here are some practical strategies you can try:

Set Clear Boundaries: If you work in an office or share a workspace with others, consider setting boundaries that can minimize distractions. For example, you may want to politely inform your colleagues that you need quiet time to focus and ask them to respect this by limiting interruptions during certain hours of the day. Similarly, you may want to set specific times to check your email and respond to messages instead of doing so haphazardly throughout the day.

Use Noise-Canceling Headphones: If you find that background noise is impeding your focus, consider investing in a good pair of noise-canceling headphones. These headphones can block out distracting sounds and help you maintain your concentration.

Break Up Your Work: It can be challenging to stay focused for extended periods, even when working on something you enjoy. One effective strategy is to divide your work into small, manageable tasks and take breaks in between. For example, you can work for 45 minutes and then take a 10-15 minute break to recharge your brain.

Minimize Screen Time: Social media, emails, and instant messaging can be a significant drain on your time and attention. Try to limit the amount of time you spend scrolling through your phone or checking your email. Set specific times throughout the day to catch up on your notifications and commit to staying off your phone during focused work periods.

Practice Mindfulness: Finally, incorporating mindfulness practices like meditation or deep breathing can help you cultivate greater awareness and focus. Try to take a few minutes each day to sit quietly and focus on your breath or body. You may find that this helps you build mental resilience and hone your ability to concentrate for more extended periods.

These are just a few practical strategies you can try to overcome distractions and maintain your focus. Remember, each person is unique, and what works for one introverted brain may not work for another. So, take some time to experiment with different techniques and see what works best for you. With practice, you can harness the power of your focus and achieve your goals with greater ease and efficiency.

Creative Breaks: How to Refuel Your Energy and Creative Juices

As introverts, we require time alone to recharge and think deeply. However, we cannot always have that luxury, especially if we are in a demanding job or situation that demands constant output. Fortunately, there are ways to take creative breaks that do not require complete isolation.

One effective method is to engage in activities that spark our curiosity and deepen our interests. For example, when we are in the midst of a challenging project, taking a few minutes to read about a related topic can bring innovative ideas and insights.

Another approach is to move our bodies. By doing so, we release endorphins and other neurochemicals that promote well-being, reduce stress, and enhance cognitive performance. A brisk walk, stretch or even dancing for a few minutes can be an effective way to re-energize us.

In addition to physical activity, some introverts find that

taking a quiet moment, like meditation or deep breathing, can help us clear our mind and refocus. These moments of stillness can also help us tune in to our inner selves, which can lead to creative, intuitive insights.

Finally, it is essential to know when to step away and take a more extended break. If we have been working tirelessly for hours, taking a power nap or a more extended walk can give us the mental break we need to return to work more productively.

As introverts, we may seem like we need to work tirelessly without stopping, but taking these creative breaks and recharging our batteries is vital to our well-being and can fuel our creativity and productivity in the long run.

The Power of Flow: How to Achieve Deep States of Concentration and Productivity.

As an introvert, your ability to focus may be one of your most powerful assets. While extroverts may enjoy bouncing between conversations and activities, you have the unique ability to concentrate intensely on a single task or topic. Harnessing this power of focus can lead to deep states of concentration and productivity, which is often referred to as "flow."

Flow is a state of mind where you are fully immersed in the activity or task at hand, experiencing a sense of energized focus, full involvement, and enjoyment. When in flow, time seems to fly by and distractions fade away. This highly focused state can lead to increased creativity, problem-solving, and productivity.

To achieve flow, there are a few key elements that need to be in place. First, the activity or task should be challenging but not too difficult. It should push you just outside of your comfort zone, but not so far that it becomes frustrating or overwhelming. Second, you need to have a clear goal in mind and receive immediate feedback on your progress. This helps you stay focused and motivated. Third, eliminate distractions as much as possible. Close your email and silence your phone. Lastly, be fully present in the moment, without worrying about past or future events.

As an introvert, you may find it easier to achieve flow than extroverts since you already have a natural inclination towards concentration and introspection. However, it's still important to recognize the importance of flow and make it a priority in your life. Set aside time each day for tasks that require deep focus and try to eliminate distractions during these times. With practice, you can harness the power of flow and achieve even greater productivity and creativity in your life.

Chapter 5: Communication Mastery: Introvert-Friendly Strategies for Effective Interaction

Hone Your Listening Skills

Understanding the Power of Active Listening

Effective listening is a critical skill that introverts can use to their advantage in social interactions. Active listening involves not just hearing the words, but also paying attention to non-verbal cues and the implied meaning behind them. It requires tuning out distractions and demonstrating a genuine interest in what the other person is saying.

Introverts are naturally better listeners than extroverts, but there is always room for improvement. Active listening builds rapport and trust, allows deeper understanding of the other person, and helps reveal hidden information. People appreciate when they feel heard and understood.

The first step in active listening is to give your full attention to the speaker, with an open and non-judgmental attitude. This means setting aside any preconceived notions, biases or assumptions, and focusing entirely on the message being conveyed.

The second step is to ask questions, clarify doubts, and

paraphrase the other person's message in your own words. This helps ensure mutual understanding and also strengthens the memory of the information.

Effective listening also involves being aware of non-verbal cues such as body language, tone, and facial expressions. These subtle signals can reveal the other person's emotions and thoughts.

Active listening is a valuable skill that can enhance social interactions for introverts. By giving full attention, asking questions, and being aware of non-verbal cues, introverts can build rapport and trust, deepen understanding, and become better communicators.

Overcoming Common Barriers to Effective Listening

As an introvert, you likely have a natural inclination to listen keenly before responding. However, at times, you may struggle to retain focus and genuinely hear what others are saying. Several factors can impede effective listening, including internal and external distractions, biases, and preconceptions.

One common barrier to listening is preoccupation with preparing a response, assuming you know what the speaker is going to say before they finish. This tendency to jump ahead in anticipation can lead to confusion and miscommunication. Instead, try to shift your mindset towards listening to understand, not just to respond.

Another obstacle to effective listening is internal

distraction, such as ruminating over a personal issue, abstractly daydreaming, or fixating on a particular detail of the conversation. To overcome internal distractions, practice mindfulness and present-moment awareness. Ground yourself in the reality of the discussion instead of distracting personal thoughts or abstract ideas.

External distractions are also a common barrier to listening effectively. They can range from physical discomfort, like noisy surroundings or interruptions by others, to more subtle disturbances like a speaker's language or accent barrier. Combatting external distractions involves creating an environment that fosters effective listening. Find suitable locations for conversations, switch off notifications, and practice active listening exercises.

Finally, being aware of your biases and preconceptions can improve your listening ability. Suppose you hold strong beliefs about a particular topic or person; you may have more difficulty hearing alternative perspectives. Instead, approach each conversation with a receptive and open mind. Listen carefully to the other person's point of view and avoid categorizing them based on inherent biases.

By identifying and addressing these barriers to effective listening, you can sharpen your ability to communicate meaningfully and cultivate authentic connections.

Developing Empathy to Connect with Others

Effective communication is not just about conveying your own thoughts and ideas, but also about understanding the perspectives and needs of those around you. This requires developing empathy, the ability to put oneself in someone else's shoes and understand their feelings and experiences.

For introverts, who tend to be more introspective and reflective, developing empathy may come more naturally than for their extroverted counterparts. However, it is still important to actively work on cultivating this skill.

One way to develop empathy is to practice active listening. This means giving the speaker your full attention, avoiding interrupting or judging, and asking clarifying questions to ensure you understand their message.

Another technique is to use visualization to put yourself in someone else's position. Imagine their circumstances, feelings, and motivations, and try to empathize with what they may be experiencing.

In addition, it can be helpful to seek out diverse perspectives and experiences through reading, traveling, or engaging in meaningful conversations with individuals who come from different backgrounds.

By developing empathy, introverts can not only improve their communication skills but also deepen their connections with others and foster more meaningful relationships.

Strategies for Improving Your Listening Skills

In this section, we'll explore specific strategies for improving your listening skills as an introvert. As introverts, we often prefer to listen and observe in conversations rather than jump in and dominate the discussion. But active listening is a key component of effective communication, regardless of whether you're an introvert or an extrovert.

Firstly, it's important to remove any distractions that may take your focus away from the speaker. This means turning off your phone or putting it on silent, making eye contact with the speaker, and eliminating any other potential distractions in your environment.

Next, try to focus on what the speaker is saying, rather than formulating your response while they're still speaking. This can be a difficult habit to break, but it can have a significant impact on the quality of your interactions.

Another strategy is to ask open-ended questions that encourage the speaker to share more information about their thoughts and experiences. This can demonstrate your interest in what they're saying and help you become more engaged in the conversation.

Lastly, summarizing and reflecting back what you've heard is another effective way to improve your listening skills. Not only does this demonstrate that you're actively engaged in the conversation, but it also provides an opportunity to clarify any misunderstandings and strengthen the connection between you and the speaker.

By employing these strategies, introverts can hone their listening skills and become more effective communicators.

Leveraging Your Strengths as an Introverted Listener

As an introvert, you have a natural ability to listen and

absorb information. You often observe more than you speak and carefully consider before responding. These are the strengths that you can leverage to become a better listener and communicator.

Firstly, learn to pay attention to body language and tone of voice in addition to the speaker's words. Your attentiveness to non-verbal cues can give you a deeper understanding of what the speaker is trying to convey.

Secondly, practice active listening by asking open-ended questions and reflecting on what the speaker is saying. This will show that you are engaged and interested, and it will also help you to clarify any misunderstandings.

Thirdly, use your reflective thinking skills to think deeply about what you hear. Synthesize the information, apply it to your prior knowledge, and develop new insights. This will help you to come up with thoughtful responses that demonstrate both your listening skills and your intellectual abilities.

Lastly, remember that listening and speaking are two sides of the same coin. By being a great listener, you will gain more information and insights, which will equip you to speak more confidently when the time comes. Be proud of your introverted strengths and use them to become a great listener and communicator.

Speaking with Confidence

Accepting Your Voice: A Guide to Overcoming Self-Doubt

As an introverted person, it's natural to doubt your ability to communicate effectively, whether it's during a presentation, a meeting, or even in a one-on-one conversation. However, it's important to recognize that your voice matters and that you have valuable insights to offer.

The first step towards speaking with confidence is accepting your voice. This means understanding that your personality, experiences, and perspectives are unique and valuable, and that you have just as much right to speak up as anyone else.

One way to overcome self-doubt is by preparing ahead of time. If you have a meeting or presentation coming up, take the time to gather your thoughts and organize them in a way that makes sense to you. Write down key points or ideas you want to communicate, and practice saying them out loud.

Another strategy is to focus on your strengths. Introverts tend to be great listeners, thinkers, and observers, which can be incredibly valuable in communication. For example, if you're part of a group discussion, take the time to listen actively to what others are saying, think about the points they're making, and offer a thoughtful response based on your insights.

It's also important to be authentic and true to yourself when communicating. Don't try to force yourself to be someone you're not, or to adopt an extroverted communication style that doesn't feel natural to you. Instead, find ways to communicate in a way that feels comfortable and authentic.

Ultimately, speaking with confidence is about recognizing your value and your ability to contribute to conversations and discussions. By accepting your voice and focusing on your strengths, you can overcome self-doubt and communicate effectively as an introverted person.

Crafting Your Message: Strategies for Effective Communication

In the previous section, we discussed the importance of vocalizing your thoughts and ideas confidently, especially in professional settings. However, rushing to speak up without having a well-crafted message can potentially damage your credibility and impact. In this subsection, we will delve into strategies to help you structure and deliver effective messages when communicating with others.

One of the critical steps in crafting your message is having a clear goal of what you want to achieve through your communication. Start by identifying the purpose of your message, whether you want to inform, persuade, or entertain your audience. Clarifying your intention can help you tailor your message to your audience's needs and interests, making it easier to communicate confidently and effectively.

Next, it's essential to organize your thoughts cohesively. A structured message is easier to follow and comprehend, reducing the risk of losing your audience's attention. Begin by outlining the key points you want to emphasize in your message, and arrange them in a logical flow. This helps you avoid unnecessary repetition or tangents, ensuring your message stays on track.

Another crucial aspect of crafting your message is using appropriate language and tone. You may need to adjust your language and tone depending on your audience's level of expertise, familiarity with the topic, and the message's purpose. Be mindful of the words you use and the way you construct sentences. Use simple and precise language to convey your message's essence, avoiding jargon or technical terms that may be unfamiliar to your audience.

Finally, it's useful to practice and refine your message delivery. Start by rehearsing alone and then in front of a test audience, preferably someone you trust to give you honest feedback. During your practice sessions, pay attention to your body language, pace, and tone. Try to maintain eye contact with your audience, speak clearly and confidently, and adjust your pace to keep your audience engaged.

By developing these skills, you can gain the confidence and ability to craft and deliver compelling messages, enabling you to communicate more effectively in any scenario.

Building Awareness of Nonverbal Communication

In any interaction, nonverbal communication plays an integral role in conveying our feelings and emotions, especially for introverts who are more comfortable communicating through nonverbal cues. Recognizing and utilizing nonverbal communication can help introverts project confidence, credibility, and authority during communication.

Eye contact is a crucial nonverbal cue; it shows that you are paying attention and engrossed in the conversation. For some introverts, maintaining eye contact can be challenging, but with time, practice, and pushing oneself out of the comfort zone, it can become second nature.

Body language also plays a crucial role in communication. Being aware of how one is perceived is important. It helps introverts understand how they are coming across and adjust their body language accordingly. Avoid slouching and crossed arms, as they can signal a lack of interest or defensiveness.

Facial expressions are another aspect of nonverbal communication that can communicate emotions and moods. Smiling, nodding, and maintaining a generally pleasant demeanor can create a positive atmosphere and encourage others to engage in conversation.

Lastly, introverts should pay close attention to the tone of their voice. It is not only what one says, but how one says it that matters. Speaking slowly and articulately can convey confidence and thoughtfulness, while avoiding monotone or excessively soft-spoken delivery can keep the listener engaged.

Through building awareness and practicing nonverbal communication, introverts can become more effective communicators, projecting confidence and authenticity that can deliver great results.

Using Your Introverted Strengths to Enhance Your Speaking Skills

Introverts may assume that their quiet nature makes them poor speakers, but in reality, introverts can utilize their unique strengths to become powerful and effective communicators. Here are some ways introverts can use their natural tendencies to enhance their speaking skills:

Preparation and Research:
Introverts tend to be thorough and thoughtful in their approach to tasks. This same trait can be used to prepare for speaking opportunities. Take time to research and gather information to ensure that you are well-versed in the topic at hand. Use your inclination to introspect to analyze the message you want to convey and how you can communicate it effectively.

Reflective Listening:
Introverts tend to be good listeners. This quality can be helpful when speaking as well. Before speaking, take a few deep breaths and listen to the tone and pace of the conversation around you. This can help you tailor your message to the audience, and ensures that your message connects with them.

Use of Storytelling:
Introverts often connect with others through storytelling. Focusing on using illustrations and stories in your communication can help connect with the audience on an emotional level. This makes it easier for the audience to remember the important points.

Take Time to Respond:
Introverts tend to think things through before responding.

103

Instead of seeing this as a hindrance, you can use this trait to your advantage. Take a few moments to process the information before articulating your thoughts to make sure your message is clear and concise.

Embrace Your Unique Style:
Most importantly, do not try to emulate an extroverted style when communicating. Introverts can be extremely effective communicators when they are authentic to their natural strengths, such as thoughtfulness or deep listening. Embrace your quiet nature, use your preparedness, reflective listening, storytelling, and thoughtful responses, to create a powerful communication style that is uniquely your own. By doing so, you will stand out and leave a lasting impression with your audience.

Managing Your Nerves and Anxiety When Speaking

Public speaking can be daunting for anyone, but it seems especially challenging for introverts, who may prefer the comfort of solitude over addressing a large group of people. This anxiety can stem from a fear of being judged, saying something wrong, or being the center of attention for too long. However, with the right mindset and techniques, introverts can overcome their nerves and deliver an engaging and confident presentation.

Shift Your Thinking
The first step to managing your nerves when speaking in public is to shift your thinking from fear to excitement. Embrace the challenge of sharing your thoughts and ideas with others and remind yourself that you are an expert on

the topic you are presenting.

Practice, Practice, Practice
The more you practice your speech, the more confident and prepared you will feel. Practice in front of a mirror, record yourself, or rehearse with a trusted friend or colleague. By getting more familiar with your material, you can focus on delivering your message and engaging with your audience, rather than worrying about what you're going to say next.

Visualize Success
Visualization is a powerful tool that can help calm nerves and boost confidence. Imagine delivering a successful, engaging presentation and receiving positive feedback from your audience. This will help you build confidence and prepare for any potential challenges you may face.

Take Deep Breaths
When you're feeling nervous or anxious, your body may react with shallow breathing or holding your breath. Take a few deep breaths before you start speaking to calm your body and mind. This will help you speak more clearly and confidently.

Start Small
If the thought of speaking in front of a large group is too overwhelming, start with smaller audiences or less formal settings. Volunteer to speak in a class, at a team meeting, or at a community event. This will help you build confidence and experience, and you can gradually work your way up to larger, more high-stakes presentations.

By employing these techniques and shifting your mindset, introverts can become powerful communicators and confident speakers. Remember, public speaking is a skill that can be learned and developed with practice and patience.

Navigating Group Conversations

The Challenges of Group Communication for Introverts

Group conversations can be daunting for introverts. They often feel overwhelmed in large social gatherings and prefer more intimate settings. In group conversations, it can be challenging for introverts to find their space and contribute to the conversation. This subsection will discuss some of the challenges of group communication for introverts.

A. Feeling Overpowered

In group conversations, extroverts often dominate the conversation space. They tend to be louder and more confident, which can make introverts feel overwhelmed and overshadowed. It can be difficult for introverts to assert themselves in conversations and share their thoughts and ideas.

B. Difficulty Processing Information

Introverts require time to process information and formulate their thoughts. In group conversations, the pace of the conversation can be fast, leaving very little time for introverts to collect their thoughts and respond. This can be frustrating and make introverts feel isolated and excluded from the conversation.

C. Feeling Disengaged

Group conversations often involve superficial and small-talk topics that may not interest introverts. When not interested, introverts tend to disconnect and become disengaged from the conversation, which can further isolate them from the others in the group.

D. The Fear of Being Judged

Introverts are often self-conscious and worry about how they are perceived by others. They may be reluctant to offer their opinions in group conversations for fear of being judged or criticized by others. This fear can hold introverts back and keep them from fully participating in the conversation.

E. Feeling Exhausted

Group conversations can be draining for introverts. The noise, the multiple voices, and the need to navigate social dynamics can be exhausting. Introverts recharge their energy by spending time alone, so extended periods of group conversation can leave them feeling mentally and emotionally depleted.

Group conversations can present challenges for introverts. They may struggle to assert themselves, process information, engage with the topics, deal with their fears, and manage their energy levels effectively. However, by understanding the challenges and adopting some introvert-friendly strategies, introverts can learn to navigate group conversations with greater ease and confidence.

Strategies for Managing Group Conversations

Group conversations can be intimidating for introverts,

especially when there are many people participating. However, with the right strategies, introverts can effectively participate and even lead group conversations. Here are some tips for managing group conversations as an introvert:

Set clear goals for the conversation: Before the conversation begins, it's helpful to have a clear understanding of what needs to be accomplished. This can help keep the conversation focused and prevent it from becoming overwhelming for introverts.

Use active listening: When in a group conversation, it's important to actively listen to what others are saying. This means paying attention to their words, tone, and body language. Active listening can help introverts better understand the conversation and contribute meaningfully.

Take breaks when needed: Group conversations can be draining for introverts. It's okay to take a break and step away from the conversation when needed to recharge and gather your thoughts.

Use your strengths: As an introvert, you may be more comfortable observing and analyzing situations before responding. Use this strength to your advantage by taking time to reflect before contributing to the conversation.

Speak up when necessary: Although introverts may prefer to listen and observe, there will be times when it's necessary to speak up and contribute to the conversation. Practice assertiveness and be confident in your ideas and opinions.

By using these strategies, introverts can effectively navigate and contribute to group conversations. Remember, introversion is a unique strength, and introverts have valuable insights and perspectives to share.

Making the Most of Your Participation in Group Discussions

As an introvert, group discussions may not be on the top of your list of favorite activities. However, effective communication in a group setting can be an essential skill in both personal and professional contexts. The following strategies can help you make the most out of your participation in group discussions.

Firstly, be prepared. If you know that you will be involved in a group discussion, take some time to prepare ahead of time. Create an outline of the points you want to make, and practice expressing them to yourself or a trusted friend. Having a clear understanding of your thoughts and ideas can help you express them more effectively in the group discussion.

Secondly, actively listen. It's easy to tune out when you're not the one speaking, but being an active listener can help you contribute more effectively to the conversation. Try to really focus on what the other participants are saying and genuinely engage with their ideas. This will make it easier to respond to their points and build upon them with your own contributions.

Thirdly, find your moments. Group discussions can often be dominated by the loudest and most outspoken participants. As an introvert, it's important to be strategic about when you step into the conversation. Look for natural lulls in the conversation or points where you have particular expertise, and use these moments to jump in and make your contributions. You don't need to speak up at every opportunity, but making thoughtful and well-timed contributions can make a big impact on the group discussion.

Fourthly, don't be afraid to follow up. In a group discussion, it's easy for important points to get lost or for discussions to move quickly from one topic to the next. If there's a point that you want to emphasize or an idea that you want to explore further, don't be afraid to follow up after the discussion is over. This could mean sending an email, scheduling a follow-up meeting, or simply approaching the person individually to continue the conversation. By taking the initiative to follow up on key points, you'll show that you're engaged and committed to the group's goals.

By implementing these strategies, you can ensure that your participation in group discussions is effective and impactful, even as a naturally quiet introvert.

Techniques for Leading Group Discussions as an Introvert

As an introvert, it can be challenging to facilitate group discussions, especially when you are expected to take charge of the conversation. However, leading group discussions is an excellent opportunity for introverts to showcase their unique strengths.

Here are some introvert-friendly techniques that can help you lead group discussions effectively:

Prepare in advance: Take time to prepare for the discussion so that you feel confident and comfortable leading the group. Make sure you have a clear idea of the discussion topics and any points you want to cover.

Encourage participation: As an introvert, you may not feel comfortable dominating the conversation. Encourage other group members to participate by asking open-ended questions and inviting them to share their thoughts.

Active listening: Practice active listening during the discussion. Listen carefully to what other group members are saying, and make sure you understand their points. Repeat or rephrase their statements to show that you are engaged and interested.

Pacing and timing: Control the conversation's pacing and timing so that everyone has a fair opportunity to speak. It can help if you set a time limit for each topic and use a timer to keep everyone on track.

Focus on the group's objectives: Keep the discussion focused on the group's objectives and goals. Refocus the discussion if it begins to wander off-topic.

Use nonverbal communication: Use nonverbal cues such as nodding, eye contact, and facial expressions to signal that you are engaged and listening to the group's contributions.

Leading group discussions may seem daunting at first, but with practice, even introverts can become effective facilitators. By using these techniques, you can take advantage of the opportunity to showcase your strengths as an introvert and lead the group to success.

Sustainable Strategies for Participating in Group Conversations without Burning Out.

As introverts, group conversations can be overwhelming and exhausting. However, avoiding them entirely is not always an option, especially in professional settings. Here are some sustainable strategies for participating in group conversations without burning out:

Set realistic goals: Before entering a group conversation, decide on a realistic goal for your participation. It could be to share one thought or idea, or to actively listen and contribute to the discussion in a small way. By doing this, you can establish a clear purpose for your participation and avoid feeling overwhelmed.

Find a comfortable physical space: Group conversations can be noisy and chaotic, which can exacerbate introvert anxiety. Finding a comfortable physical space in the conversation can help ease this anxiety. Consider sitting next to someone you know well, or sitting in a corner with your back against the wall.

Take breaks when needed: It's okay to take breaks during a group conversation, especially if you feel overwhelmed or anxious. Step away for a few minutes to recharge, or ask to step out for a phone call or bathroom break.

Use non-verbal communication: If speaking up in a group conversation feels uncomfortable, try using non-verbal communication. This can include nodding, making eye contact, or using hand gestures to show agreement or understanding.

Focus on quality over quantity: It's not always necessary to contribute to every aspect of a group conversation. Instead, focus on contributing quality ideas or thoughts when you feel comfortable doing so. This can help you avoid feeling overexerted while still maintaining a valuable presence in the conversation.

Navigating group conversations can be challenging for introverts, but with these strategies, it is possible to participate comfortably and sustainably.

Chapter 6: Networking for Introverts: Building Connections Without Burning Out

Understanding the Networking Landscape

The Importance of Networking for Introverts

Networking is often seen as an extrovert's game, where the most gregarious person in the room walks away with the most connections. But as an introvert, you can still benefit from networking if you approach it in the right way.

In fact, networking could be even more crucial for introverts since they typically prefer deep and meaningful connections over surface-level interactions. Building and cultivating genuine relationships is essential, both personally and professionally.

As an introvert, it's easy to fall into the trap of thinking that your work should speak for itself, and networking is just a distraction from that. However, no matter how talented you are, it's unlikely that people will come to know or appreciate your work unless you put yourself out there. Networking can help you find the right opportunities or collaborators, get support or feedback, and even boost your career prospects.

Moreover, building relationships with fellow introverts or like-minded people can be incredibly enriching. You may find that others share your perspectives and passions, leading to fulfilling conversations and collaborations. This can especially be beneficial if you're looking for mentorship, guidance or inspiration.

So don't be hesitant to dive into networking as an introvert. With the right approach, it can be a powerful investment in your personal growth and impact.

The Myths and Misconceptions of Networking

In today's world, networking has become an essential part of life. It can be a great opportunity to make connections, promote yourself or your business, and explore new opportunities. However, for introverts, networking can be a daunting task. There are several myths and misconceptions surrounding networking that can discourage introverts from participating. In this section, we will debunk these myths and discuss how introverts can overcome their networking fears.

One common misconception is that networking is only for extroverted people. This is far from the truth. While extroverted people may find networking more natural, introverts too can be excellent networkers. The critical thing is to understand your strengths and use them to your advantage. Introverts can be excellent listeners, which is an essential attribute of successful networking.

Another myth is that networking is all about collecting business cards and making small talk. While this is part of networking, it is not what makes it successful. Networking should be about building relationships and lasting connections. Introverts can achieve this by focusing on quality over quantity. Instead of trying to make small talk with several people, introverts can direct their effort towards building meaningful conversations with a few people.

A common fear for introverts is that they will have nothing to contribute to the conversation. However, introverts are often good at asking questions and listening attentively. This can lead to them making more thoughtful contributions to the conversation than their extroverted counterparts.

Furthermore, introverts may feel overwhelmed by networking events and the large crowds of people. It is important to remember that networking is not just limited to events. It can also happen over coffee, lunch, or through online platforms. Introverts can seek out smaller, more intimate gatherings or one-on-one conversations to build relationships.

Networking is a skill that all introverts can develop. By understanding their strengths, focusing on quality over quantity, and seeking out more intimate gatherings, introverts can build meaningful relationships through networking.

The Different Types of Networking Events

Networking events come in all shapes and sizes, each with its own unique challenges and opportunities. For introverts, it's essential to choose events that align with their strengths and interests. In this section, we'll explore the different types of networking events and offer tips for making the most of each one.

Professional Association Events - These events are held by industry-specific associations to provide professional development, networking, and learning opportunities for their members. These events are geared more towards individuals already established in their respective fields and are looking to expand their professional network. For introverts, these events are ideal because everyone in attendance shares the same professional interests, making it easier to find common ground and start a conversation.

Trade Shows and Conferences - Trade shows and conferences are large-scale, industry-specific events that bring together professionals from various sectors to showcase products, services, and innovations. Conferences or conventions are events where attendees attend workshops, presentations, and seminars to learn more about a specific industry or topic. These events offer multiple opportunities to network and learn new skills, but they can be overwhelming for introverts. To navigate these events successfully, you must plan your schedule in advance, research and prioritize the sessions you want to attend, and be strategic in your networking approach.

Meetups and Informal Gatherings - Meetups and informal gatherings are organized by people with shared interests who want to socialize or learn something new. They are typically less formal than professional association events or conferences, and they allow for more organic connection-building. For introverts, meetups are prime networking opportunities as you can choose groups that align with your interests, making it easy to find common ground and start conversations.

Social Events - These events are based on activities like sports, games, art or music. They are also platforms to socialize and meet people with diverse interests. Introverts struggle in such events because they don't want to be the center of attention. But they could look up for activities that they are interested in and that include fewer people, in order to feel comfortable.

Networking events come in different forms, and introverts may have different preferences. It is important to understand which events will complement your strengths and interests, prioritize and plan accordingly. By doing this, you can make the most out of each event and build a network that suits your needs.

Finding Networking Opportunities That Align with Your Interests

As an introvert, networking may often seem daunting and overwhelming, but understanding what you are looking for can make all the difference. Finding networking opportunities that align with your interests is crucial, as it can make it easier to engage and participate in conversations.

One way to start is by reflecting on your goals and interests. Do you have a passion or hobby that you enjoy? Are you interested in a particular industry or subject? Once you have identified your interests, you can start looking for events and groups that cater to those areas.

Networking events can take various forms, such as

conferences, seminars, workshops, or online communities. You could follow industry experts on social media or attend meetups, which are informal gatherings focused on specific topics or interests. Look for opportunities where you can connect with like-minded individuals and find common ground to discuss.

It is also helpful to research the organizations hosting the events to get an idea of their culture and values. Are they focused on education and mentorship, or are they more sales-focused? Understanding the philosophy behind the event can help you prepare and tailor your approach to match the environment and individuals you may meet.

When attending events, try to approach them with a growth mindset, rather than a transactional one. Instead of thinking about how you can benefit from the event immediately, focus on building relationships and learning from others. Try to engage in meaningful conversations, ask open-ended questions, and listen actively.

Finding networking opportunities that align with your interests is a great way to make connections and build meaningful relationships as an introvert. By identifying your goals and focusing on events that cater to your passions, you can alleviate some of the anxiety that comes with networking and create a more enjoyable and fulfilling experience.

How to Prepare for Networking Events

In order to successfully network as an introvert, preparation is key. Here are some tips for preparing for a networking event:

Do Your Research - Before attending a networking event, research the event and the attendees. This will help you identify potential conversation topics and prepare thoughtful questions to ask.

Set Goals - Set realistic goals for yourself before the event, such as meeting a certain number of people or exchanging contact information with someone in your industry.

Plan Your Outfit - Choose an outfit that makes you feel comfortable and confident. This will help you feel more at ease during the event and allow you to focus on networking.

Arrive Early - Arriving early can help you feel more comfortable in the space and give you time to settle in before the event begins.

Bring Business Cards - Having business cards on hand can make it easier to exchange contact information and follow up with new connections after the event.

Take Breaks - Networking can be overwhelming, especially for introverts. Remember to take breaks throughout the event to recharge, whether that means stepping outside for a few minutes or finding a quiet corner to collect your thoughts.

By taking the time to prepare for networking events, introverts can feel more confident and capable in social situations.

Mastering the Networking Event

How to Make a Great First Impression

As introverts, networking events can often feel overwhelming and intimidating. The thought of having to introduce ourselves to strangers and make small talk can be enough to make us want to avoid such events altogether. However, mastering the art of making a great first impression is a fundamental skill that can help put us at ease and set the tone for successful networking.

The key to making a great first impression is to be authentic and genuine. Rather than putting on a false persona or trying to be someone we're not, it's important to showcase our unique strengths and personality. This can help us stand out from the crowd and make a lasting impression.

One way to do this is to prepare ahead of time. Going into a networking event with a clear sense of our goals and objectives can help us stay focused and confident. We can also think about how we want to introduce ourselves and what key points we want to convey, such as our professional experience, interests, or areas of expertise.

Another important aspect of making a great first impression is body language. Research shows that nonverbal cues such as eye contact, posture, and tone of voice play a significant role in how others perceive us. By practicing good posture, maintaining eye contact, and speaking clearly and confidently, we can convey a sense of competence and professionalism.

Finally, it's important to remember that making a great first impression is only the first step in building a lasting relationship. Following up with contacts after the event, whether through email or social media, can help solidify the connection and keep the conversation going. By staying true to ourselves and our strengths, and taking the time to prepare and practice, introverts can excel at networking events and build lasting relationships that can help further our personal and professional goals.

Approaching and Starting Conversations

In social and professional gatherings, it's essential to be able to approach and initiate conversations. It's an important skill, especially for introverts, who may feel intimidated or overwhelmed by the idea of networking. However, when done right, opening a conversation can lead to an enjoyable and fruitful meeting.

To begin with, it's crucial to observe the people around you and try to identify those who seem approachable. Perhaps someone is standing alone or appears to be looking for someone to talk to. Approaching them would be the best way to initiate a conversation, and it may also help you feel more in control of the situation.

When you approach someone, it's essential to keep in mind that they may also be hesitant or unsure about networking. That's why it's important to be confident and friendly. A simple "hello" or "how are you doing today?" can break the ice and start a conversation. It's also essential to maintain eye contact and smile genuinely.

Another way to initiate a conversation is by using open-ended questions. These types of questions encourage dialogue rather than a simple yes or no answer. For example, asking "What brings you to this event today?" or "What do you think about the speaker's presentation?" can lead to a more engaging discussion. It's important to follow up with further questions to show that you're interested in the conversation.

When entering a conversation that's already underway, it's essential to join in without interrupting or disrupting the flow. It's also essential to be aware of the body language of the people in the conversation. Are they open and engaged or closed-off and disinterested? It's important always to approach with respect and not to force yourself into the conversation.

Approaching and starting a conversation at networking events can be a daunting task for introverts. However, by observing the people around you, being confident and friendly, and using open-ended questions, you can initiate a conversation and create a more enjoyable and productive networking experience.

Active Listening and Engaging in Meaningful Conversations

As an introvert, networking events can be overwhelming and stressful. But they don't have to be. With the right strategies, you can master the networking event and build meaningful connections without feeling burned out.
One of the most important skills introverts can develop for successful networking is active listening. It's not just about

hearing what the other person is saying; it's about truly engaging with them and understanding their perspective.

To become an active listener, start by giving the person your full attention. Maintain eye contact and avoid distractions, such as checking your phone or scanning the room for other people. Listen to what they are saying and ask follow-up questions to show that you are interested and engaged. Stay present in the moment, and avoid interrupting or assuming you know what the person is going to say next.

Another key aspect of active listening is being open-minded and non-judgmental. Avoid jumping to conclusions or dismissing someone's ideas before you fully understand them. Instead, strive to see things from their perspective and find common ground for a deeper connection.

Engaging in meaningful conversations is also crucial for building connections at networking events. To do this as an introvert, it can be helpful to prepare some conversation starters or questions in advance, such as asking about the person's background or their interests. You can also read up on recent news, industry trends, or common topics related to the event to have something to discuss.

Remember, networking events are not about collecting as many business cards as possible, but about building genuine connections with people. By actively listening and engaging in meaningful conversations, you can find common ground and build relationships that will benefit you and your career in the long run.

Introducing Yourself and Making Your Pitch

After understanding the networking landscape and preparing for the event, it's time to dive into mastering the art of the networking event itself. For many introverts, the thought of going to a networking event can be daunting, but with some preparation, it can be a successful and enjoyable experience.

Once you arrive at the networking event, it's time to start making connections. The first step in doing so is introducing yourself in a clear and concise manner. It's essential to have a solid elevator pitch - a brief, persuasive speech that describes who you are, what you do, and what you are seeking. The key is to keep it simple, memorable, and genuine.

One common mistake introverts make is trying to sound too formal or professional, which can come off as disingenuous. Instead, aim for authenticity and speak from the heart. Share your passion and the value you bring in a way that resonates with the listener.

Next, be sure to actively listen to the person you are speaking to. Introverts tend to excel at this, but it's essential to remind yourself to focus on the person you're speaking with, not simply wait for your turn to talk. Ask thoughtful questions and engage in meaningful dialogue. By doing so, you'll build rapport and establish a solid foundation for a lasting relationship.

Finally, remember that networking isn't just about acquiring business cards - it's about building meaningful connections. Keep the conversation light and enjoyable, and don't be afraid to share personal experiences or interests if they align with the person you are speaking with. The goal is to create a memorable experience that leaves a lasting impression.

Mastering the art of introducing yourself and making your pitch at networking events is essential for building connections as an introvert. By preparing a strong elevator pitch, actively listening, and keeping the conversation authentic and enjoyable, you can overcome the fear and anxiety of networking and build fulfilling and successful relationships.

Ending Conversations and Building Connections for the Future

As an introvert, networking events can be difficult to navigate. While you may be able to start conversations with ease, ending them can be a challenge. However, it is essential to learn how to end a conversation and build connections for the future. Here are some strategies to help you do just that:

Express gratitude: As the conversation comes to a close, express your appreciation for the other person's time and insights. Thank them for speaking with you, and let them know you enjoyed the conversation. This simple gesture goes a long way in building a positive relationship.

Exchange contact information: Before ending the conversation, be sure to exchange contact information. This can include business cards or social media profiles, depending on your preference. Make sure to follow up after the event to keep the connection alive.

Have a plan: Before attending a networking event, have a plan in place for the conversations you want to have and the people you want to meet. This can help you prioritize your time and ensure you make meaningful connections.

Be authentic: As you end the conversation, be sure to stay true to yourself. Don't force a connection or try to be someone you're not. Authenticity is key to building lasting relationships.

Make a statement: If you want to continue the conversation or potentially work together in the future, make a statement that expresses your interest. You might say, "I would love to continue this conversation sometime" or "Let's grab coffee and talk more about this."

Remember, networking events are not just about collecting business cards or making small talk. It's about building meaningful relationships that can benefit you and others in the future. By ending conversations gracefully and building connections for the future, you can successfully navigate networking events as an introvert.

Building and Sustaining Relationships

Nurturing New Connections: Follow-up Strategies

After attending a networking event, introverts often feel relief that the event is over but dread at the thought of following up with the connections they made. However, nurturing these connections is important for building lasting relationships. Here are some introvert-friendly follow-up strategies:

Personalize your message: When following up with a new connection, it's important to personalize your message. Mention something specific that you talked about at the event or something you learned from them. This shows that you were paying attention and are genuinely interested in continuing the conversation.

Use a medium you're comfortable with: While email is the most common medium for following up, it's not the only option. If you prefer phone or even a handwritten note, use that instead. The important thing is that you reach out and continue the conversation.

Don't wait too long: It's important to follow up within a few days of meeting someone. This ensures that the conversation is still fresh in both of your minds and shows that you're serious about developing the connection.

Be specific about next steps: When following up, it's a good idea to suggest specific next steps to continue the conversation. This could be grabbing coffee, attending another event together or just setting up a time to chat on the phone. Being specific shows that you're invested and committed to developing the relationship.

Nurturing new connections can be intimidating for introverts, but with these follow-up strategies, it can be made easier and more effective. Remember that building genuine relationships takes time and effort, but it's worth it in the long run.

Maintaining Relationships Through Technology

Introverted individuals can find it challenging to maintain close relationships with others because of their preference for solitude and quiet time. However, maintaining strong connections is important for both personal and professional growth. Fortunately, technology can be an introvert's ally in building and maintaining relationships.

The importance of social media: Social media has revolutionized the way people communicate, and introverted individuals can take advantage of these platforms to remain connected without feeling overwhelmed. Social media allows for low-pressure interactions with friends, family, and colleagues, making it an ideal tool for introverts who struggle with face-to-face communication.

Email and chat services: Email and instant messaging services can be a great way for introverts to maintain relationships with others. These tools allow for asynchronous communication, meaning introverts can take their time to carefully compose responses without feeling rushed or pressured. Additionally, people are generally more candid in writing than in face-to-face conversations, so introverts may find that they can forge deeper connections through these means.

Virtual hangouts: Virtual hangouts offer a unique opportunity for introverts to connect with others without leaving the comfort of their own homes. Video chats, online gaming, and other virtual social activities provide a way to interact with others while maintaining a sense of control over the social environment.

Tips for maintaining relationships online: While technology can be a valuable tool for maintaining relationships, it's important to use it wisely. Introverts should be intentional about their online interactions and take steps to build deeper connections. Some tips for maintaining relationships through technology include regularly scheduling virtual meetups, being honest and open with communication, and actively seeking out shared interests or activities. By keeping these tips in mind, introverts can maintain strong relationships with others, even from a distance.

Building Your Network Online: LinkedIn and Beyond

In today's digital age, networking is no longer limited to in-person interactions. Online networking platforms have become increasingly popular, allowing individuals to build and maintain professional relationships with ease. For introverts, this can be a more comfortable and less energy-draining option than traditional networking events. In this subsection, we will explore the benefits of online networking and how introverts can leverage them to expand their network and advance their careers.

One of the most popular online networking platforms is LinkedIn. With over 700 million users worldwide, LinkedIn has become a key tool for job searching, showcasing one's skills and expertise, and building professional relationships. Introverts can use LinkedIn to their advantage by curating a strong profile that highlights their strengths and experience. This can help to attract potential network connections and job opportunities without the need for extensive networking events.

To make the most of LinkedIn, introverts should also engage in active networking strategies on the platform. This involves regularly connecting with new individuals, joining relevant groups and discussions, and reaching out to potential employers or industry leaders. One approach that can work well for introverts is to focus on building a smaller network of quality connections rather than connecting with a large number of individuals without building meaningful relationships.

In addition to LinkedIn, there are plenty of other online networking platforms that can be fruitful for introverts. For instance, Twitter can be a useful tool for following thought leaders in a particular industry and engaging in conversation with them. Facebook groups can also provide a forum to connect with individuals who share similar professional interests.

As with any form of networking, it is important for introverts to set reasonable goals and maintain authenticity in their online interactions. By building relationships gradually and within their comfort zone, introverts can use online networking platforms to build a robust and valuable network that can help them succeed in their professional lives.

The Importance of Giving Back: Making Connections on Your Terms

As introverts, we often approach networking events with caution and apprehension. We may feel uncomfortable in large groups or struggle to make small talk with strangers. However, networking is an essential part of professional and personal growth, and we cannot afford to ignore it.

Thankfully, introverts have unique strengths that they can leverage to build and sustain meaningful relationships. Unlike extroverts, who thrive on constant stimulation and interaction, introverts prefer to go deep rather than wide, and they excel at listening and empathizing with others.

In this section, we will explore the importance of giving back and making connections on your terms. For introverts, networking can be a draining and exhausting activity. However, when we approach it with a mindset of service and generosity, it can become a meaningful and fulfilling experience.

One way to give back is by connecting people with shared interests or goals. As introverts, we have a keen eye for detail, and we can often spot potential synergies and opportunities that others miss. By playing the role of a connector, we can add value to our network and help others achieve their goals.

Another way to give back is by sharing your expertise and knowledge. Introverts often have a deep understanding of their areas of interest, and they can use this knowledge to help others. By offering insights and advice, we can establish ourselves as a thought leader and create a lasting impression on others.

Finally, giving back can also mean simply showing up and being present. As introverts, we may feel overwhelmed by large groups or unfamiliar settings. However, by showing up and being fully present, we can build trust and rapport with others. This can lead to meaningful connections and opportunities down the road.

Giving back is an essential part of networking for introverts. By approaching networking with a mindset of service and generosity, we can build and sustain meaningful relationships that enrich our lives both professionally and personally.

Managing Burnout and Maintaining an Effective Networking Practice

As an introvert, it's essential to realize that networking can be an energy-draining activity, leading to burnout if you're not careful. In this subsection, we'll explore strategies to manage burnout effectively and maintain an effective networking practice.

One approach is to focus on quality over quantity. Building relationships takes time and effort, so instead of trying to network with as many people as possible, make a conscious effort to connect with a smaller group of individuals consistently. This level of consistency will reduce the need for ongoing outreach and leave more time for authentic conversations.

Another strategy is to prioritize self-care. Being an introvert means that downtime is critical. Build breaks into your day or take a step back from networking events and opportunities when you're feeling overwhelmed. Try to schedule networking events during periods where you feel the calmest or less overloaded.

It's also important to recognize when it's time to say no. Know your limits and set realistic expectations for yourself. If a networking opportunity isn't aligned with your objectives, politely decline. Be mindful of your energy reserves, and don't feel compelled to attend every event, party or meeting because you'll end up more exhausted than energized.

The final strategy in managing burnout is to track progress. By recording the successes, no matter how small, through note-taking or a gratitude journal, you will realize the progress you have made. By acknowledging your progress, you build confidence and strengthen your motivation.

Chapter 7: Thriving in an Extroverted World: Navigating Social and Professional Landscapes

Mastering Social Events

Recognizing Your Limits: Setting Goals for Social Events

As an introvert, social events can be daunting and overwhelming. It's essential to recognize your limits and set realistic goals for each event you attend. Before attending any social event, reflecting on your energy levels and mood is crucial. Be honest with yourself and ask if you have any social energy left. If you've had a long day, it might be best to skip the party altogether.

While setting goals, it's essential to remember that it's okay to step out of your comfort zone, but it's not okay to push yourself past your limits. Start by setting small and achievable goals. For instance, you could aim to stay at the event for one hour instead of five hours. Additionally, setting specific goals like joining a conversation with two people can make it easier to take action.

It's important to remember that everyone at the event is there for a specific purpose, and you're no exception. If you're struggling to find your place, consider finding an activity that aligns with your hobbies or interests. It could be a games night or a book club. There's bound to be an activity that feels right for you.

Setting goals for social events can make them less daunting and overwhelming. Be honest with yourself and set achievable goals. Remember that everyone at the event is there for a purpose, and you belong there too. Find an activity that aligns with your interests, and enjoy yourself.

Preparing for Social Events: Setting Scenes and Grounding Expectations

As an introvert, the thought of attending social events may cause anxiety and stress. However, with the right preparation and mindset, these events can be more manageable and even enjoyable. In this section, we will discuss ways to set the scene and ground expectations before attending social events.

It's important to remember that social events are not designed solely for extroverts. There are many other individuals, including other introverts, attending these events as well. Therefore, it's crucial to approach social events with an open and positive mindset.

Before attending a social event, take time to prepare yourself mentally and physically. Ensure that you have enough rest and relaxation time in the days leading up to the event. Additionally, consider carving out some time for meditation, deep breathing, or any other mindfulness practice to help ground yourself in the present moment.

Setting specific goals and expectations can also help manage anxiety and stress. For example, if attending a networking event, you might set the expectation to meet at least three new people and get their contact information. By having a clear objective in mind, you can approach the event with more confidence.

Lastly, consider bringing a trusted friend or colleague to the event. Having a familiar face can provide a sense of comfort and ease any apprehension about attending.

By taking the time to prepare and set goals, attending social events can become a source of growth and personal fulfillment rather than a source of stress and discomfort.

Making Connections: Small Talk and Beyond

Small talk is an unavoidable aspect of social events, and it can be especially daunting for introverts. However, mastering the art of small talk can be a powerful tool for building relationships and making connections.

Firstly, it's important to recognize that small talk shouldn't be dismissed as meaningless chatter. It serves a vital function in laying the groundwork for more meaningful conversations. To make small talk less intimidating, introverts can prepare some simple questions or conversation starters ahead of time. These could relate to the event or the setting, such as "Have you tried the appetizers yet?" or "How was your commute here?"

When engaging in small talk, introverts should strive to actively listen to the other person and show genuine interest in their responses. This can be demonstrated through follow-up questions or comments that demonstrate that you are engaged in the conversation. For example, if someone mentions that they just returned from a trip, ask them a question about their experience or offer a comment related to their destination.

Beyond small talk, introverts can make deeper connections by engaging in conversations that genuinely interest them. This can involve seeking out like-minded individuals or attending events that cater to your interests. Additionally, introverts can build connections by offering their expertise or assistance to others. This can be done by volunteering to help out with a specific task or offering your knowledge in a particular area.

Ultimately, introverts should view social events as an opportunity to connect with others on a deeper level. By reframing small talk as a powerful tool for relationship-building and seeking out conversations that align with their interests, introverts can thrive in social settings and build meaningful connections with others.

Dealing with Awkwardness: Conversation Stoppers and Recovery Techniques

It's happened to all of us at some point – a conversation stalls, and you're not quite sure what to say next. You feel awkward, and the silence seems to stretch on forever. As an introvert, this can be especially challenging, as we tend to be more sensitive to social cues and can easily become overwhelmed by uncomfortable situations. But fear not – there are ways to recover from conversation stoppers and turn the tide in your favor.

First, it can be helpful to recognize some common conversation stoppers. These can include topics that are uncomfortable or controversial, or simply running out of things to talk about. If you find yourself in this situation, try to shift the focus and steer the conversation in a new direction. This might mean asking a question about the other person's interests or sharing a personal experience that relates to the topic at hand.

Another strategy is to use humor to diffuse the tension. A well-timed joke or witty comment can help break the ice and lighten the mood. Just be sure to keep it appropriate and respectful, as humor can also be a potential conversation stopper if not used thoughtfully.

If all else fails, it's okay to simply acknowledge the awkwardness and move on. Sometimes the best thing to do is to own up to the situation and transition to a new topic or politely excuse yourself.

Remember, conversation stoppers are a normal part of social interaction, and everyone experiences them from time to time. The key is to develop the confidence and resilience to handle these situations with grace and ease. With practice and patience, you can become a master at navigating even the most challenging social events.

Exiting Gracefully: Wrapping Up Social Events with Confidence

As an introvert, attending social events can be daunting. However, mastering the art of leaving social events gracefully can be just as important as handling the event itself. Here are some tips for exiting social events with confidence:

Plan your exit strategy: Before even attending the event, plan out your exit strategy. Decide what time you want to leave and how you will make your departure.

Show gratitude: Before leaving, make sure to thank the host for inviting you and express your enjoyment of the event.

Say goodbye to important individuals: If there were specific individuals you spent time with at the event, make sure to say goodbye and thank them for the conversation.

Don't over-explain: When saying goodbye, keep it simple and gracious. You don't need to give a detailed explanation for why you are leaving, simply say that you need to get going.

Have a backup plan: In case you get stuck in conversation or can't leave as planned, have a backup plan in place. Perhaps you can excuse yourself to use the restroom one last time before making your exit.

Remember, there's no need to feel guilty for leaving a social event early. As an introvert, it's important to prioritize your own needs, and sometimes that means exiting gracefully and with confidence.

Excelling in a Professional Setting

Understanding Workplace Dynamics: Identifying Your Role on the Team

As an introvert in the workplace, it can be challenging to navigate the intricacies of office politics and team dynamics. However, it is essential to understand your role on the team to contribute effectively.

Firstly, identify your strengths and how they can add value to the team. Introverts tend to be good listeners, problem-solvers, and creative thinkers, making them valuable assets in any workplace. Understanding what you bring to the table can help you assert yourself confidently and make significant contributions to the team.

Secondly, observe how your team functions, the roles and responsibilities of each member, and how they interact with each other. Knowing your colleagues' strengths, weaknesses, and communication style can help you adapt your approach to collaborate effectively.

Lastly, identify any communication barriers inhibiting teamwork and work to address them. Introverts' preference for solitary work, for example, can sometimes be misinterpreted as disinterest, leading to misunderstandings. Clarifying expectations and communicating your needs can help you build strong relationships, promote productivity, and foster a positive team culture.

By understanding workplace dynamics, recognizing your strengths, and adapting your communication style, you can confidently contribute to your team's success while remaining true to your introverted nature.

Communicating with Confidence: Strategies for Effective Communication

Effective communication is one of the essential skills required to excel in a professional setting. However, introverts tend to struggle with it as they prefer to think before they speak and are less likely to engage in small talk. Nevertheless, there are some strategies that can help introverts communicate effectively:

Understand your communication style: As an introvert, knowing your communication style is crucial. It helps you leverage your strengths, overcome your weaknesses, and communicate more effectively. By understanding your communication style, you can communicate in a way that feels natural while still being effective.

Practice Active Listening: Being present, paying attention, showing interest, asking questions, and reflecting on what a person has said are the elements of active listening. It allows you to understand what someone is saying, respond appropriately and build stronger relationships.

Prepare before communication: Introverts tend to be more thoughtful, reflective and enjoy preparing before a communication event. Preparing ahead of any conversation or meeting helps introverts to get their thoughts and ideas organized, making them feel more confident and comfortable.

Know when to pause: Introverts tend to think before they speak, choosing their words carefully, and sifting through their thoughts. Therefore, taking the time to collect their thoughts and allowing a pause during a conversation or presentation, communicates a level of competence, thoughtfulness, and attention.

Choose your words mindfully: Introverts tend to be more precise and thoughtful about language than extroverts. You need to choose words that resonate with you, and that conveys your intended message effectively. This results in more direct and straightforward communication, whereby you can express yourself more effectively and achieve desired outcomes.

Networking with Purpose: Making Connections in the Professional World

As an introvert, the thought of networking and building professional connections may seem daunting. But the truth is, it can be just as important for introverts as it is for extroverts. The key is to approach networking with purpose and intention.

First and foremost, it's important to establish your goals and what you hope to achieve through networking. Are you hoping to find a mentor, job opportunities, or simply expand your professional network? Once you have a clear understanding of your objectives, you can begin to target specific events and individuals to help you achieve them.

When attending networking events, focus on quality over quantity. It can be tempting to try to meet as many people as possible, but forming deeper connections with a few individuals can be more beneficial in the long run. Identify individuals whom you admire or whom you believe could offer valuable insights or opportunities, and make a genuine effort to connect with them.

One approach to networking that may feel more comfortable for introverts is to attend smaller, more intimate events or to set up one-on-one meetings with professionals in your field. This can provide a more relaxed and focused environment for meaningful conversations.

It's also important to remember that networking doesn't always have to take place in formal settings. Keeping in touch with former colleagues or classmates, engaging with professionals on social media, and participating in online forums can also be effective ways to build connections and expand your network.

Ultimately, the key to networking as an introvert is to be authentic, intentional, and strategic in your approach. Don't try to be someone you're not or force yourself into uncomfortable situations. Instead, play to your strengths and focus on building relationships that align with your goals and values.

Managing Time and Energy: Balancing Work and Personal Needs

As an introvert, managing time and energy can be a challenging task, especially when it comes to balancing work and personal needs. Time management can be more challenging for introverts who recharge their energy differently from extroverts. To excel in a professional setting, it's crucial to understand your energy levels and how to optimize your productivity.

Understanding Your Energy Levels

To manage your time and energy effectively, you need to understand your energy levels. Some introverts tend to have higher energy levels in the morning, while others find their energy spikes in the afternoon or evening. Understanding your energy patterns will help you schedule your most challenging tasks during your high-energy periods.

Prioritizing and Planning Your Workday

To balance your work and personal needs, prioritize your workday by creating a to-do list. Prioritizing your tasks based on their importance and urgency will help you accomplish more in less time. Breaking down larger tasks into smaller ones and tackling them one by one can also help reduce overwhelm and increase productivity.

Taking Breaks and Resting

To prevent burnout, it's crucial to take breaks and rest throughout the day. As introverts recharge their energy by alone time, it's essential to take time alone during breaks. Find a quiet spot to recharge, listen to music or read a book, and avoid taking breaks with colleagues who drain your energy. Setting boundaries and taking care of your energy levels will help you sustain your productivity while avoiding exhaustion.

Time-Blocking and Scheduling

To manage time and energy effectively, try time-blocking and scheduling challenging tasks during high-energy periods. Scheduling non-negotiable breaks throughout the day will help you maintain your energy levels, prevent burnout and increase productivity. By taking control of your time, you can optimize your workday, accomplish more in less time, and thrive in your professional life.

Managing your time and energy as an introvert can be challenging and taxing, but by understanding your energy patterns, prioritizing, taking breaks, and scheduling effectively, you can excel in your professional life while balancing your personal needs.

Moving Forward: Career Advancement Strategies for Introverts

As an introvert, the idea of advancing in your career may seem daunting. You might feel like you're at a disadvantage because the business world tends to favor those who are more outgoing and assertive. But fear not! There are strategies that you can implement to help you excel in your chosen profession.

A. Find Your Niche: Identify your Strengths and Passion

One of the keys to excelling in your career is to find your niche. Identify your strengths and passions, and look for ways to apply them in your work. This will not only make you more productive and fulfilled, but it will also make you more valuable to your employer.

B. Take Initiative: Seek Out Opportunities

Don't wait for opportunities to come to you. Take the initiative and seek them out. Express your interest in taking on new projects, attending trainings or conferences, and pursuing new certifications or degrees. This shows your employer that you are enthusiastic about your job and are committed to your professional development.

C. Build Relationships: Networking and Mentoring

Networking and mentorship are vital components of career advancement. As an introvert, you may find networking challenging, but remember that it's not about making small talk or being the life of the party. Rather, it's about building relationships and developing connections that can help you further your career.

Find a mentor who can provide guidance and support as you navigate the workplace. Look for networking opportunities that align with your interests and strengths, such as joining professional organizations or attending industry events.

D. Communicate Effectively: Speak Up and Advocate

Introverts tend to be great listeners and observers, which can be an asset in the workplace. However, it's also important to speak up and advocate for yourself when necessary. Learn to communicate effectively, whether it be in meetings, presentations, or one-on-one conversations with your supervisor.

E. Create Your Own Path: Embrace Your Uniqueness

Finally, remember that you don't have to follow the traditional path to career advancement. As an introvert, you have unique qualities and strengths that can set you apart from others. Embrace your uniqueness, and find ways to make it work to your advantage.

Take the time to reflect on what you want to achieve in

your career, and then create a plan that works for you. Remember, there's no "right" way to advance in your career – it's up to you to create your own path to success.

Navigating Extraverted Environments

Recognizing Extraverted Behaviors: Understanding the Needs of Extraverts

As introverts, it is easy for us to become overwhelmed in excessively extraverted environments, feeling as though we do not belong. This section of the chapter will aim to rectify that by exploring the understanding of extraverted behaviors, thereby making you recognize the needs of extraverts.

Without presuming you to be an expert on extraverted behavior, it is necessary to introduce you briefly to the concept of extraversion. Extraverts are people who react to stimuli by being more outgoing, talkative, and sociable in their behaviors than introverts. They crave interactions and social attention, whereas introverts prefer being alone or in groups of familiar people.

One important thing to note here is that extraverts do not necessarily seek to dominate conversations or interrupt others. They are just wired to process external stimuli more actively than introverts. In an extroverted environment, it is essential to understand and appreciate such features to avoid coming across as aloof or unfriendly.

Another thing to note is that extraverts can be fascinating conversationalists, capable of sparking engaging and exciting dialogues. They thrive on external feedback and are drawn to environments that provide external stimulation. However, considerate extraverts can tone down their energy levels to accommodate introverts, and likewise, we can learn to adapt to their needs as well.

Understanding extraverted behaviors is vital to navigating through extraverted environments without losing a sense of self. It does not require adopting their ways but merely appreciating their energy and enthusiasm while staying true to our introverted selves.

Setting Boundaries: Establishing Limits and Saying "No"

Navigating extraverted environments as an introvert can be a daunting task, especially when it comes to setting boundaries. It is important to establish limits that help you maintain a balance between social obligations and personal time. Saying No is one of the most challenging but essential parts of setting boundaries. It can be hard to resist the pressure to attend every social event or work-related activity, but learning when and how to say "No" is crucial for your mental health and wellbeing.

One of the first steps to setting boundaries is to assess which activities are most important to you, and which ones drain your energy. It can be helpful to approach social events and professional obligations with a clear idea of your priorities, so you can prioritize your time and energy accordingly. If you have a work event that feels essential, for example, you may decide to attend but skip socializing at the after-party to ensure you have enough energy for the next day.

Another essential step in setting boundaries is to communicate your needs clearly and directly. While it can be challenging, especially if you are not used to saying no or feel like you might disappoint someone, communicating your needs directly is crucial. Use assertive language that represents your needs, rather than using vague or ambiguous statements that may be easily dismissed. If someone invites you to a social gathering, for example, you might say, "Thanks for inviting me, but I think I need an evening in to recharge," rather than "I'm not sure if I can make it."

It can be helpful to establish patterns and routines that help you protect your personal time. For example, you might decide to keep your weekends free for personal time, or to only schedule one event per week. You might also create habits that help you recharge, like reading a book or going for a walk after work. Establishing healthy patterns and communicating your needs can help you navigate extraverted environments in a way that works for you, without compromising your own wellbeing.

Coping with Overwhelm: Managing Stress and Avoiding Burnout

As an introvert, navigating an extraverted environment can be overwhelming and stressful, leading to burnout. However, there are ways to manage the stress and avoid burnout. One way is to set limits for yourself. It's essential to know your limits and not spread yourself too thin. It's okay to say no to events or projects that you can't handle. Additionally, it's important to take time for yourself. Carve out time in your day to do something that relaxes you, whether it's reading a book or going for a walk. Make self-care a priority.

Another way to cope with overwhelm is to plan ahead. This

means creating a schedule and sticking to it. By planning your day, you will know what to expect, and it will give you a sense of control. Planning ahead also means giving yourself enough time to recharge after a social or professional event. This could mean taking a day off work or scheduling some downtime before and after the event.

It's also helpful to have a support system. This could be friends, family, or a therapist. Having people who understand your introverted nature and can offer support and encouragement can make a significant difference.

Finally, it's essential to reframe your mindset. Instead of seeing extraverted environments as a threat, try to view them as an opportunity for growth. Use these events as a chance to challenge yourself and step out of your comfort zone. Celebrate your accomplishments, no matter how small they may seem. Reframing your mindset can help to reduce stress and boost confidence.

Coping with overwhelm in extraverted environments requires setting limits, self-care, planning ahead, having a support system, and reframing your mindset. With these strategies, you can manage stress, avoid burnout, and thrive in an extraverted world.

Maintaining Authenticity: Remaining True to Yourself in Extroverted Environments

As an introvert, it can be extremely challenging to maintain authenticity in an extroverted environment. It's important to remember that being truc to yourself is essential for your mental and emotional well-being. However, it's easy to fall into the trap of trying to conform to the norms of an extraverted world.

One way to maintain authenticity is by setting boundaries. Be clear about what you're comfortable with and what you're not. For example, if you don't like attending large social events, don't force yourself to go. Instead, find other ways to connect with people that feel more authentic to you, such as one-on-one conversations.

Another important factor is communication. Be honest with others about your introverted nature and how it affects your interactions. It's okay to let them know that you may need some alone time to recharge, or that you prefer to communicate via email rather than in-person.

It's also important to remember that introverts have unique strengths and perspectives that can be valuable in an extroverted environment. Don't be afraid to share your ideas and insights with others. Your quiet confidence can be a powerful asset in situations where others may be more quick to speak without fully considering all options.

Finally, practice self-care. Taking the time to recharge and reflect is essential for introverts to maintain their authenticity and prevent burnout. Whether it's reading a book, taking a long walk, or simply sitting in quiet contemplation, make sure to prioritize your own needs and well-being.

Navigating an extroverted world can be challenging for introverts, but by setting boundaries, communicating honestly, embracing your strengths, and practicing self-care, you can maintain authenticity and thrive in any environment.

Thriving in Your Own Way: Embracing Your Introverted Nature in an Extroverted World

Navigating extroverted environments can be challenging for introverts, but it's possible to thrive and succeed by embracing your introverted nature. In this subsection, we'll look at some strategies for staying true to yourself and finding success in an extroverted world.
As an introvert, it's important to remember that you don't have to change who you are to succeed in an extroverted world. Instead, focus on identifying your strengths and finding ways to use them to your advantage.

One of the most important things you can do is to create opportunities for alone time. This might mean taking breaks during the day to recharge, or scheduling downtime after a busy week to give yourself a chance to rest and reset.

You can also leverage your natural listening skills to help build connections with others. By listening carefully and asking thoughtful questions, you can show others that you value their perspectives and ideas, which can lead to stronger relationships and more meaningful conversations.

Another strategy for thriving as an introvert in an extroverted world is to find ways to showcase your strengths in meaningful ways. This might mean taking on leadership roles that allow you to work independently and make a significant impact, or finding ways to demonstrate your expertise through writing, speaking, or other means.

Ultimately, the key to thriving as an introvert in an extroverted world is to stay true to yourself and to approach challenges with an open mind and a willingness to try new things. By embracing your introverted nature and finding creative ways to leverage your strengths, you can achieve success and fulfillment in any social or professional landscape.

Chapter 8: The Introverted Leader: Harnessing Your Quiet Strengths for Effective Leadership

Understanding Introverted Leadership

Embracing Your Quiet Strengths

As an introverted leader, your quiet strengths are the key to your success. By embracing your introverted nature, you can tap into unique qualities that can make you a more effective leader. These strengths include your ability to listen deeply, your tendency to think before you speak, and your aptitude for working independently.

One of the most significant advantages of introverted leadership is the ability to listen carefully. Introverts have an exceptional capacity for active listening, which can be invaluable when it comes to building strong relationships with their team members. By taking the time to truly hear what others have to say, introverted leaders can create a sense of trust and respect that is essential for effective collaboration.

Introverted leaders also have a natural tendency to think before they speak, which can be a valuable asset in any leadership role. By taking the time to consider all angles of a situation, introverted leaders can make more thoughtful decisions that are less likely to be influenced by emotions or external pressures.

Finally, introverted leaders excel at working independently. In today's fast-paced and often chaotic work environments, the ability to stay focused and self-directed can be a real advantage. Introverted leaders are less likely to be distracted by external stimuli or peer pressure, and are more likely to have the self-discipline and focus necessary to see complex projects through to completion.

The key to harnessing your quiet strengths as an introverted leader is to embrace and leverage your unique qualities. By recognizing the value of your listening skills, thoughtful approach, and independent nature, you can become an effective and respected leader in any context.

The Value of Listening

As an introverted leader, one of your greatest strengths lies in your ability to listen. Introverts tend to be excellent listeners, and this skill can be incredibly valuable in a leadership role.

In a world where extroverted qualities like charisma and assertiveness are often rewarded, introverts may feel like they are at a disadvantage. However, the ability to listen and take in information can be just as important as being able to speak confidently and take charge.

When you listen carefully to your team members, you gain valuable insights into their perspectives, ideas, and concerns. This information can help you make better decisions, build stronger relationships, and create a more productive and harmonious work environment.

Listening also demonstrates your respect for your team members and their contributions. When you take the time to actively listen to what they have to say, you show them that you value their input and that they are important members of the team. This can help build a more positive and supportive team culture.

To become a better listener, it's important to practice active listening techniques. This means focusing your attention fully on the speaker, maintaining eye contact, and avoiding distractions like phones or emails. It also involves asking thoughtful questions and reflecting back what you've heard to ensure that you understand the speaker's message clearly.

As an introverted leader, your quiet strength can be a powerful tool in building a successful team. By valuing and honing your listening skills, you can harness your unique leadership style and make a positive impact in your organization.

Creating Safe Spaces for Collaboration

As introverts, we have an innate ability to listen and observe, which can be the foundation for successful group collaborations. However, group settings can also be overwhelming for introverts, who may struggle to assert themselves in noisy and chaotic environments. Therefore, creating a safe and structured space for collaboration can help introverted leaders harness their unique strengths and foster a productive and creative team culture.

One way to achieve this is by establishing clear communication protocols to ensure that everyone's voice is heard. This can involve setting aside specific times for group discussions and creating an agenda to keep the conversation on track. Additionally, introverted leaders can encourage team members to share their views through written communication, which not only allows for more thoughtful responses but also provides a platform for introverts to contribute without feeling anxious or overshadowed.

Another essential component of creating safe spaces for collaboration is acknowledging individual differences, including personality traits and communication styles. Introverted leaders can use tools such as personality assessments and team-building exercises to encourage team members to understand each other's strengths and differences. By doing so, introverted leaders can create a welcoming and inclusive team environment that allows everyone to feel valued and appreciated.

Introverted leaders have unique strengths that can be harnessed to create effective and collaborative teams. Creating safe and structured spaces for group discussions, acknowledging individual differences, and utilizing clear communication protocols are essential strategies for introverted leaders to foster productive and inclusive team cultures.

Empathy in Leadership

As an introverted leader, one of your most valuable assets is your ability to empathize with others. Empathy is a key component of emotional intelligence, and it enables you to understand and connect with the feelings and perspectives of your team members.

Empathy helps you to build trust and establish strong relationships with your colleagues. When you take the time to understand their needs and concerns, you can tailor your leadership approach to suit their preferences and help them to succeed.

However, empathy is not always easy to cultivate. As an introvert, you may struggle to connect with others on an emotional level. You may also find it challenging to express your own emotions and motivations in a way that is clear and compelling.

To develop your empathy skills, it is important to practice active listening and communication. This involves paying close attention to what others are saying, asking questions to clarify their meaning and intent, and responding in a way that shows you value their perspective. You can also practice reflecting on your own emotions and experiences, which can help you to better understand and relate to others.

Using empathy in your leadership approach can have significant benefits for both you and your team. By focusing on building strong relationships and connecting with your colleagues, you can create a more positive work environment and achieve greater success as a team. With practice and dedication, you can hone your empathy skills and become a more effective, confident, and influential leader.

Building Trust with Authenticity

As an introverted leader, building trust is one of the most important aspects of maintaining a sustainable and productive team. Introverts tend to prioritize authenticity in relationships and interactions in their personal and professional lives. This quality can help them create meaningful connections with their colleagues and employees.

Building trust takes time, patience, and authenticity. Authentic leaders know their strengths and limitations, and they do not hesitate to admit when they make a mistake. Employees appreciate honesty and vulnerability from their leaders, which can result in a strong bond between employees and their supervisors.

Authenticity also comes from being true to oneself. Introverted leaders who try to emulate extroverted qualities can come across as inauthentic or disingenuous. They need to embrace their unique strengths and lead in a way that feels natural to them.

To build trust with authenticity, introverted leaders should prioritize active listening and open communication. These qualities help keep lines of communication open between the leader and the team, and promote a sense of transparency and accountability.

Effective communication requires that leaders not only listen but also ask questions and respond thoughtfully, showing empathy and understanding to the people who report to them. It's important that managers and supervisors take the time to create a true connection with their employees by sharing their own personal experiences and engaging in regular feedback sessions.

Authentic leadership fosters collaboration and innovation, and encourages employees to contribute their ideas and perspectives without fear of criticism or judgment. The best leaders know how to harness the strengths of their team and leverage that power to drive success. As such, authenticity should be one of an introverted leader's greatest tools- it can lead to a more productive and harmonious workplace environment.

Overcoming Challenges as an Introverted Leader

Speaking Up and Asserting Your Voice

As an introverted leader, one of the biggest challenges you might face is speaking up and asserting your voice in a group setting. You might have brilliant ideas, but find it hard to express them amidst the noise and chaos of a meeting or discussion.

It is crucial to recognize that the ability to speak up doesn't equate to the volume of your voice. You can assert your voice and make impactful contributions without compromising your introverted nature.

One strategy to help you speak up is to prepare ahead of time. If you know there will be a meeting or discussion, take the time to gather your thoughts and ideas beforehand. Write them down and practice expressing them. By doing so, you'll be able to articulate your points more clearly when the time comes.

Another effective technique is to find a way to engage in the conversation that feels comfortable for you. You could speak up early on, when the discussion is just beginning and the environment is less overwhelming. You could also seek out a smaller, more intimate group setting, where you feel more comfortable expressing yourself.

Additionally, it's essential to remember that you don't have to speak up in every conversation or meeting. As an introvert, you may have a unique perspective that others might not think of. Instead of focusing on speaking up all the time, try to identify the moments where your input will be particularly valuable.

Finally, don't underestimate the power of active listening. As you listen actively to others, you'll be able to identify common themes and offer insights that build on what others have said. This approach can be particularly effective for introverts as they often prefer to reflect and think before speaking.

Speaking up and asserting your voice as an introverted leader can be challenging, but it's a critical skill to develop. Focus on preparing ahead of time, finding comfortable situations to engage in, identifying key moments to contribute, and active listening to build on others' ideas. By doing so, you'll be able to make meaningful contributions and assert your voice without compromising your introverted nature.

Addressing Confrontation and Conflict

Introverted leadership comes with unique challenges, one of which is confrontation and conflict. This is a challenge for most introverts as they tend to avoid these situations due to the levels of stress and anxiety they induce. However, as a leader, it is essential to address confrontation and conflict head-on, or else productivity, team morale, and progress can be hindered significantly.

Introverted leaders should understand that confrontation and conflict are not always negative but, rather, necessary components of a productive and successful team. It is crucial to approach these situations with an open mind, calm demeanor, and objectivity. This means understanding the different perspectives, being attentive to evidence and facts, and avoiding taking situations personally.

As an introverted leader, it is vital to learn how to communicate effectively during confrontations and conflicts. This means that they should be careful with their word choices, tone, and body language to ensure that their message is communicated effectively while avoiding escalation. The use of active listening, empathy, and validation are also critical components during such situations.

One way of addressing confrontation and conflict as an introverted leader is by accessing their quiet strengths, such as strategizing, careful planning, and thoughtful decision-making. Through this approach, introverted leaders can devise solutions that satisfy everyone involved in the conflict while keeping the peace.

Another approach is to seek assistance or guidance from extroverted members of the team. While introverted leaders may find it challenging to handle confrontations and conflict, extroverted team members tend to thrive in such situations. Therefore, seeking their input can provide clarity on different perspectives and possible solutions.

Addressing confrontation and conflict as an introverted leader is possible. However, it requires objectivity, effective communication skills, accessing their quiet strengths, and seeking input from other team members. By doing so, introverted leaders can create a productive and successful team.

Navigating Networking Events and Public Speaking

Public speaking and networking are essential skills for leadership roles in any industry. They require effective communication skills, charisma, and the ability to connect with people on a personal level. For introverted leaders, these activities can be incredibly challenging and draining.

However, with the right mindset and preparation, introverted leaders can navigate networking events and public speaking engagements with confidence and ease. Here are some tips to help you overcome these challenges:

Plan and Prepare: The key to successful public speaking and networking is preparation. Take the time to research the audience, understand the topic, and practice your delivery. Prepare a script or talking points that will help you stay on track and ensure that you are clear and concise.

Embrace Your Style: Don't try to be someone you're not. Embrace your introverted nature and use it to your advantage. Focus on your strengths, such as your attention to detail, listening skills, and ability to connect with others on a deeper level. Use these skills to engage with your audience in a way that is authentic and meaningful.

Practice Active Listening: As an introvert, you may not be the most vocal person in the room, but you can still be an effective communicator by practicing active listening. Pay attention to what others are saying and ask thoughtful questions. This will help you build stronger connections and establish trust and credibility with your audience.

Take Breaks: Networking events and public speaking engagements can be exhausting for introverts. Take breaks between conversations or speeches to recharge and refocus. Find a quiet corner where you can collect your thoughts and recharge before returning to the event.

Celebrate Your Successes: Finally, don't forget to celebrate your successes. Public speaking and networking can be challenging, but with practice and perseverance, you can overcome these challenges and excel as an introverted leader. Recognize your achievements and give yourself credit for your hard work and dedication.

Building a Strong Support System

Effective leadership is not just about personal strengths and capabilities, but also about having a strong support system. For introverted leaders, building a solid support system is essential in overcoming the challenges they face.

One important aspect of building a support system is identifying trustworthy individuals who can provide constructive feedback and guidance. These individuals can be mentors, coaches, or colleagues who understand and respect introverted tendencies. Regular interactions with these individuals can help the introverted leader gain insight into their own strengths and areas for improvement, and help them navigate complex leadership challenges.

Another critical aspect of building a support system is creating a network of peers and colleagues who provide a sense of social support and camaraderie. By joining professional groups or attending networking events, introverted leaders can expand their social circle and forge strong, meaningful relationships with others in their field. These connections can provide valuable insights, resources, and opportunities for growth and development.

In addition to external support, introverted leaders also need to build an internal support system. This involves cultivating self-awareness and self-care practices that promote emotional and mental well-being. This may involve activities such as meditation, journaling, or engaging in hobbies or exercise. By taking care of their physical and emotional needs, introverted leaders can recharge their energy and maintain focus and clarity, even in demanding leadership roles.

Building a strong support system is essential for introverted leaders. By identifying trustworthy mentors, cultivating a network of peers, and engaging in self-care practices, introverted leaders can overcome the challenges they face and achieve success in their roles as effective leaders.

Managing Energy and Avoiding Burnout

In this section, we will explore the unique energy needs of introverts and how they can balance their energy levels to avoid burnout. Introverts tend to expend a lot of energy during social interactions and require more time to recharge. They need to carefully manage their energy levels to maintain their productivity and avoid burnout.

One-way introverted leaders can manage their energy is by creating a schedule that allows for downtime and introspection. This means consciously planning for breaks in the day, and creating an environment where people know that this time is important for their overall health and well-being. By doing so, they will be able to conserve their energy to deal with situations as they arise, without feeling drained or overwhelmed.

Another way to manage energy is to prioritize tasks according to the level of energy they require. For example, introverts may find it easier to tackle more challenging tasks early in the day when they have more energy, and schedule more routine tasks for mid-afternoon or early evening when their energy levels are lower.

Additionally, introverted leaders need to learn to say no to requests that aren't necessary or are outside their area of expertise. This means setting boundaries and not feeling obligated to be available all the time. Leaders who are introverted should be clear about their limitations, and communicate their needs in a respectful manner.

Finally, it is important for introverted leaders to find ways to recharge during the day, whether that means taking a quick walk during lunch or listening to calming music during breaks. This will help them restore their energy levels and stay focused throughout the day.

Managing energy and avoiding burnout is vital for introverted leaders to maintain their productivity and ability to lead effectively. By understanding their unique energy needs and taking steps to manage them, introverted leaders can achieve success and thrive in their roles.

Achieving Success as an Introverted Leader

Leading by Example

As an introverted leader, your ability to lead by example is one of your strongest assets. Your quiet and thoughtful demeanor can set a tone of respect and integrity, inspiring your team to follow your lead. Here are a few ways that you can harness your strengths and lead by example as an introverted leader:

Communicate with clarity: As an introverted leader, you may not be the most verbose person, but you can still communicate effectively. Instead of rambling on, take time to craft a clear and concise message. Practice active listening and focus on being present in conversations. Encourage your team to do the same.

Build trust through transparency: Introverted leaders have a tendency to be more introspective and reflective, which can make them more trustworthy. Share your thoughts and feelings with your team. Be transparent about your goals and intentions. This will show your team that you are authentic and committed to their success.

Foster a culture of collaboration: Introverts tend to work better in smaller, more intimate settings. Encourage collaboration among your team members by creating a comfortable and welcoming environment. Provide opportunities for your team to work together, and empower them to share their ideas openly.

Lead with empathy: Introverts are often more empathetic than extroverts. Use this to your advantage by leading with empathy. Take time to understand your team members' needs and motivations. Show them that you care about their success and well-being.

Learn from your mistakes: Introverts tend to be perfectionists, but this can be a double-edged sword. Use your introspective nature to learn from your mistakes and be willing to adapt your leadership style as needed. Embrace failure as a learning opportunity, and encourage your team to do the same.

By leading by example, introverted leaders can create a strong and effective team culture that drives success. With your quiet strength and thoughtful approach, you can inspire your team to be their best selves and achieve their goals.

Setting Clear Expectations

As an introverted leader, it is essential to set clear expectations for your team. Clear expectations help create a sense of direction and purpose while also ensuring that everyone is on the same page. Moreover, setting clear expectations makes it easier to hold your team accountable for their actions.

To set clear expectations, you must first determine what you want to achieve. Then, communicate those expectations to your team. When communicating expectations, be specific and use clear, concise language. Use examples and be sure to provide context to help your team understand why those expectations are important.

It is also essential to provide your team with the necessary resources to achieve those expectations. This may include providing training, tools, or support when needed. Additionally, encourage your team to share their feedback and identify any obstacles they may encounter. Encouraging open communication and feedback helps your team feel valued and respected while also promoting a culture of continual growth and improvement.

Finally, be consistent in holding your team accountable for meeting those expectations. Be willing to address any issues that arise and hold everyone to the same standard, including yourself. Consistency helps build trust and respect, which are essential for effective leadership.

Setting clear expectations is critical for achieving success as an introverted leader. By communicating clear objectives, providing necessary resources, encouraging feedback, and holding everyone accountable, you can lead your team towards success while leveraging your unique introverted strengths.

Empowering and Developing Team Members

As an introverted leader, it is essential to understand that it is not just about your own success but also about the success of your team members. Empowering and developing your team members is an integral part of achieving success as a leader.

One of the ways to empower and develop your team members is by setting clear expectations and goals. When team members know what is expected of them and have specific goals to work towards, they are more likely to stay motivated and engaged. As an introverted leader, you can communicate these expectations and goals through one-on-one conversations, emails, or messages, rather than in large group settings.

Another way to empower and develop your team members is by recognizing and utilizing their strengths. As an introverted leader, you may naturally identify the strengths and talents of your team members. Take the time to understand their strengths and provide opportunities for them to use them in their work. This can not only improve team performance but also boost morale and job satisfaction.

Offering regular feedback and coaching can also help to develop your team members. An introverted leader may prefer to provide feedback in writing or through one-on-one conversations rather than in group settings. Regular feedback, with a focus on development rather than criticism, can help team members feel supported and motivated to improve their performance.

Finally, creating a culture of psychological safety and trust within your team can empower and develop team members. As an introverted leader, you may be skilled at creating deeper connections with team members through one-on-one conversations. You can use this to create an environment where team members feel safe to express their ideas and concerns without fear of judgment or retribution. Encouraging open communication and active listening can help team members feel valued and heard.

Empowering and developing team members is crucial for achieving success as an introverted leader. Clear expectations, utilizing strengths, offering regular feedback and coaching, and creating a culture of psychological safety and trust can all contribute to the growth and development of your team members.

Leveraging Introverted Superpowers for Business Success

As an introverted leader, you possess a unique set of strengths that can propel you towards success. Your natural inclination towards thoughtful reflection and strategic planning can make you a valuable asset in the business world. Here are some introverted superpowers that can help you achieve success in your professional endeavors:

Listening and empathy: Introverts tend to be great listeners and have a heightened sense of empathy. These qualities can make you an effective communicator and team leader. By understanding your team members' needs and concerns, you can build a stronger, more cohesive team that works together towards a common goal.

Creativity and innovation: Introverts often have a rich inner world where they can tap into their creativity and imagination. This can be a huge asset when it comes to innovative problem-solving and brainstorming. By embracing your creative instincts, you can bring fresh perspectives and ideas to the table, helping your business stay ahead of the curve.

Focus and dedication: Introverts tend to be highly focused and dedicated individuals. You're likely to be meticulous in your work, paying close attention to every detail. This can make you an excellent project manager or team leader, ensuring that every task is completed to the best of your ability.

Calmness and level-headedness: In high-pressure situations, your calm and measured demeanor can be an asset to your team. While extroverts may become flustered or outspoken under stress, introverts are more likely to maintain their composure and make rational, strategic decisions.

By leveraging these introverted superpowers, you can achieve great success in the business world. Remember, being introverted doesn't mean you're weak or incapable – it means you have a unique set of talents that you can use to your advantage. By embracing your introverted nature and harnessing your quiet strengths, you can become a truly effective and successful leader.

Identifying and Pursuing Leadership Opportunities That Align with Your Values

As an introverted leader, achieving success can be daunting, but you can find it by identifying and pursuing leadership opportunities that align with your values. This can provide you with a sense of purpose and encourage you to step out of your comfort zone.

The first step in this process is introspection, learning what matters most to you, and aligning your values with your career goals. When you focus on what intrinsically motivates you, you are more likely to find fulfillment in your work. For example, if you value helping others, you may decide to pursue a leadership position in an organization that caters to your passion.

Once you have identified your values, the next step is seeking out leadership opportunities that align with them. For example, you may find a mentor who shares the same values as you and is passionate about the same goals. You can learn from their experiences and build a valuable network to support your leadership journey.

It is also essential to seek out organizations that share your values. Finding the right fit will allow you to flourish and become a successful introverted leader. When you are a part of an organization that aligns with your values, you can lead with confidence while remaining true to who you are.

Lastly, it is crucial to remember that leadership opportunities come in different forms. You do not need to have a formal leadership title to make an impact in your community. By identifying your values and what matters to you, you can make a difference in your unique way, whether it's by volunteering, mentoring others, or starting an initiative.

Achieving success as an introverted leader is not about fitting into a particular leadership style or mold. It is about reaching for opportunities that align with your values and leveraging your quiet strengths to make a meaningful impact. So, take the time to reflect on what's important to you and create a path to success that aligns with your unique self.

Chapter 9: Personal Growth: Fostering Confidence, Resilience, and Self-Acceptance

Embracing Your Unique Introverted Self

Understanding the Power of Your Introverted Traits

As an introvert, you possess a unique set of talents and abilities that set you apart from extroverts. While society often values extroverted qualities like the ability to speak up, take charge, and socialize easily, there are countless ways that introverted traits bring value to the world. Understanding your introverted strengths can help you embrace your unique qualities, build confidence, and succeed in a variety of arenas.

One key introverted trait is the ability to listen deeply. Introverts tend to be more contemplative and quiet, which makes it easier to tune in to what others are saying without feeling the need to jump in and fill the silence. This can be a valuable skill in personal and professional relationships, allowing you to build deeper connections with others by truly hearing and understanding them.

Another introverted strength is the ability to focus deeply for extended periods of time. While extroverts may thrive in fast-paced or highly social environments, introverts often excel in tasks that require sustained concentration and mental effort. Whether you're working on a complex project, honing a skill, or simply enjoying a solitary activity, you have the potential to dive deep and achieve great things through your ability to sustain your attention and perseverance.

Finally, introverts often possess a rich inner world of thoughts, feelings, and ideas. While this may cause some introverts to feel misunderstood or disconnected from others, it can also be a source of great creativity and insight. By embracing your introverted nature and allowing yourself ample time for introspection and reflection, you can tap into your inner wisdom and generate unique solutions to problems that others may not have considered.

Ultimately, understanding and embracing your introverted traits can be a powerful tool for building confidence and self-acceptance. By recognizing your strengths and valuing yourself for who you are, you can navigate the world with greater ease and achieve success on your own terms.

Overcoming Societal Pressures to Conform to Extroverted Norms

As an introvert, it's not uncommon to feel like you don't fit in with the extroverted world around you. Society often glamorizes the qualities associated with extroversion: outgoingness, gregariousness, and a love of large social gatherings. In contrast, introverts tend to value more intimate settings, reflective conversation, and quiet time for introspection.

These differences can lead to feelings of insecurity, self-doubt, and shame for introverts, who may feel like their natural tendencies are somehow deficient. This pressure to conform to an extroverted ideal can manifest in subtle ways, such as feeling self-conscious about not speaking up in a meeting or feeling like you need to force yourself to be more social than you actually want to be.

To overcome this societal pressure, it's important to recognize that there's nothing inherently wrong with being introverted. In fact, introverts bring unique strengths to the table, such as the ability to focus deeply on a task, listen attentively to others, and offer thoughtful insights.

Rather than trying to mold yourself into an extroverted version of yourself, embrace your introverted nature and find ways to work with it. For example, if you know that you don't do your best work in a crowded, noisy environment, find a quiet space where you can concentrate. If you're not comfortable in large groups, focus on building deeper connections with a few close friends or colleagues.

It's also important to recognize that there's more than one way to be a successful and fulfilled person. Society may tell us that extroversion is the preferred personality type, but in reality, introverts can thrive in a variety of fields and professions. By focusing on your strengths, identifying your passions, and pursuing work that aligns with your values, you can build a satisfying and meaningful career as an introverted person.

Overcoming societal pressures to conform to extroverted norms is essential for embracing your unique introverted self. By recognizing the value of your introverted strengths and finding ways to work with them, you can live a fulfilling and authentic life as an introverted person.

Setting Personal Goals Based on Your Authentic Self

After embracing your unique identity as an introvert, the next step is to set personal goals based on your authentic self. What kind of life do you want to lead? What are your passions and interests? By aligning your goals with your values and personality, you can achieve greater fulfillment and happiness.

Start by reflecting on your values and what truly matters to you. This will help you identify the areas of your life that align with those values. Think about what activities or projects energize you, and what drains your energy. Use this insight to guide your goal-setting process.

Next, set achievable yet challenging goals that align with your values and bring you closer to your ideal life. These goals can be related to career, personal development, relationships, or any other aspect of your life. Remember to be specific and measurable in your goal-setting.

Once you have set your goals, develop an action plan with practical steps to achieve them. Break your goals down into smaller, manageable tasks and prioritize them based on their importance. This will help you stay focused and motivated as you work towards your aspirations.

Lastly, stay accountable to yourself by tracking your progress regularly. Celebrate your successes and learn from your setbacks. Remember that personal growth is a journey, and it takes time and effort to achieve your dreams. Stay committed and keep pushing forward towards your authentic self.

Embracing Solitude as a Source of Strength

As an introvert, you likely have a natural inclination towards solitude. However, societal expectations often deem being alone as a negative trait. In this subsection, we will explore how solitude can be leveraged as a source of strength and how to embrace it as an introverted individual.

Solitude is not loneliness; it is a state of being alone without feeling lonely. While extraverts may gain energy from being around others, introverts recharge by spending time alone. Research shows that solitude can enhance creativity, promote self-awareness, and improve decision-making skills.

To embrace solitude, it's helpful to look at it as a conscious choice rather than something forced upon us. Make solitude a priority by scheduling alone time into your routine, whether it's taking a walk outdoors, reading a book, or indulging in a hobby. Use this time to reflect, recharge, and connect with yourself on a deeper level.

Furthermore, it's essential to shake off any social stigma attached to solitude. Reframe your thinking and recognize that self-reflection and introspection are crucial components in personal growth and development.

While embracing solitude may be challenging at first, it's a valuable tool for introverts to cultivate their strengths and lead a more fulfilled life. By accepting your unique nature and practicing self-care, you can tap into your full potential as a quietly confident introvert.

Developing a Positive Mindset for Long-Term Introverted Growth

As an introvert, it can be challenging to embrace your unique nature when the world around you seems to value extroversion above all else. However, it's essential to recognize the value of being an introvert and learn to appreciate your strengths. In this section, we will explore how you can develop a positive mindset that fosters long-term growth as an introvert.

A. Why a Positive Mindset is Crucial for Introverted Personal Growth
The Power of Believing in Yourself
How Negative Self-Talk Hinders Progress
Overcoming Self-Doubt and Fear of Failure

B. Strategies for Cultivating a Positive Mindset
Setting Realistic Goals
Celebrating Small Wins
Incorporating Positive Affirmations
Engaging in Self-Care Practices

C. Mindset Shifts That Can Positively Impact Introverted Growth
Embracing Mistakes and Failures as Opportunities for Growth
Recognizing the Value of Quiet Time and Solitude
Shifting Focus from External Validation to Internal Satisfaction
Embracing Challenges and Stepping Out of Your Comfort

Zone

By cultivating a positive mindset, introverts can develop the confidence, resilience, and self-acceptance needed to thrive in an extroverted world. It's a journey that requires patience, but with the right mindset, anything is possible.

Building Confidence and Resilience as an Introvert

Facing and Overcoming Introvert-Specific Challenges

Being an introvert in an extroverted world can often present specific challenges that can affect our confidence and resilience. The pressure to constantly speak up, network, and assert ourselves in social and professional situations can be daunting. However, by recognizing and addressing these challenges, we can build our confidence and resilience as introverts.

A. Overcoming Fear of Public Speaking
Public speaking is often cited as one of the top fears for people, and for introverts, the fear of speaking in public can be magnified due to our preference for solitude and introspection. However, by practicing and preparing thoroughly, introverts can learn to overcome their fear of public speaking and deliver confident and impactful presentations.

B. Navigating Small Talk and Networking
Small talk and networking events can be overwhelming for introverts, who may find it draining to constantly engage in conversation with strangers. However, by embracing our introverted strengths and focusing on deeper, meaningful connections with others, we can turn networking into a positive and productive experience.

C. Dealing with Criticism
As introverts, we may be more sensitive to criticism and feedback, which can affect our confidence and self-esteem.

However, by reframing criticism as an opportunity for growth and learning, we can develop resilience and overcome the fear of failure.

D. Setting Boundaries
Setting boundaries and prioritizing self-care is essential for introverts to maintain their energy and prevent burnout. By recognizing our limits and communicating our needs to others, we can build confidence and resilience in our personal and professional relationships.

Building confidence and resilience as an introvert may require us to challenge ourselves and step outside of our comfort zones, but by recognizing and addressing the specific challenges we face, we can cultivate a sense of self-acceptance and empowerment. Through practice and perseverance, introverts can develop the skills and confidence necessary to thrive in an extroverted world.

Developing Self-Confidence Through Self-Awareness and Reflection

When you lack confidence, it's easy to assume that others naturally possess it or that it's just not a part of who you are. But confidence is not an innate trait; it's a skill that can be developed and honed over time. One of the most effective ways to build self-confidence is through self-awareness and reflection.

Embrace your strengths and weaknesses
When you spend time exploring your internal world, you'll begin to uncover your strengths and weaknesses. This knowledge can help you embrace what you're good at and work on areas where you may struggle.

Reflect on your accomplishments
As an introvert, you're likely to let your accomplishments pass by without celebrating them fully. Take time to reflect on what you've achieved and how far you've come. Doing this can inspire self-belief and motivate you to keep going.

Journal your thoughts and feelings
Journaling is a powerful tool for building self-awareness and self-confidence. It allows you to reflect on your thoughts and feelings, untangle complex emotions, and gain clarity on what's important to you.

Set achievable goals
When you set achievable goals, you build a sense of competence and confidence. Start small and work your way up to bigger goals. Celebrate each milestone along the way, and you'll be surprised by the confidence you'll gain.

Seek feedback
As an introvert, you may shy away from seeking feedback, but it can be a valuable tool for building self-confidence. Seek feedback from trusted friends or colleagues, and use it as an opportunity to learn and grow.

Developing self-confidence takes time and practice, but with self-awareness and reflection, you can build a solid foundation for an empowered introverted life.

Navigating and Confronting Social Anxiety

As an introvert, experiencing social anxiety can be a hindrance to our daily lives. We may find that networking events, public speaking, and even small talk with colleagues can be overwhelming and draining. However, it is essential to learn how to navigate and confront social anxiety to build our confidence and resilience as introverts.

Social anxiety is a mental health condition characterized by the intense fear of social situations. It can be challenging to manage, but there are several strategies you can use to confront your anxiety and build your confidence.

One effective technique is exposure therapy, where you gradually expose yourself to anxiety-provoking situations. Start by stepping out of your comfort zone in small ways, such as striking up a conversation with a stranger or attending a social event with a friend. Over time, as you become more comfortable, you can gradually increase the level of exposure and tackle more challenging situations.

Mindfulness practices, such as meditation, can also be beneficial for managing social anxiety. Take a few minutes each day to focus on your breathing and be present in the moment. This can help you become more aware of your thoughts and emotions, allowing you to recognize and challenge any negative self-talk that may be contributing to your anxiety.

Remember, it's important to be kind and patient with yourself as you work through your social anxiety. Recognize that it's okay to feel anxious or uncomfortable in social situations, and focus on progress, not perfection. With time and practice, you can build the confidence and resilience you need to thrive as an introvert in a world that can't stop talking.

Coping with Over-Stimulation and Sensory Overload

As introverts, we often experience over-stimulation and sensory overload, especially in noisy or crowded environments. This can leave us feeling drained, anxious, and overwhelmed. In this subsection, we will explore some strategies to help you cope with these challenges and build greater resilience.

First, it's important to recognize your limits and establish boundaries that protect your energy and well-being. One way to do this is by using the "30-Second Rule." This means taking 30 seconds to check in with yourself before committing to an activity, social event, or project. Ask yourself if it aligns with your values, priorities, and energy levels. If it doesn't feel right, it's okay to say no or negotiate a compromise that works for you.

Second, practice mindfulness and self-awareness to reduce the impact of external stimuli on your nervous system. This can involve meditation, breathing exercises, or visualizations. By training your mind to focus on the present moment and filter out distractions, you can cultivate greater calm, clarity, and resilience.

Third, seek out quiet and calming environments that replenish your energy and restore your balance. This can be a park, a library, a yoga studio, or any place where you feel calm and centered. Make time for these spaces in your daily routine to give yourself the rest and recovery you need to thrive.

Finally, don't be afraid to ask for help or support when you need it. Whether it's from a trusted friend, therapist, or coach, having a support system can help you navigate challenging situations and build your confidence and resilience over time. Remember, you are not alone, and it's okay to ask for what you need to live a fulfilling, empowered life as an introvert.

Embracing Failure and Learning from Setbacks

In a society that glorifies success and achievement, failure is often seen as a taboo topic. However, it's an essential part of growth, and learning to accept and embrace it is vital for building confidence and resilience.

As an introvert, the fear of failure can be even more daunting, given our tendency to reflect and ruminate on experiences. However, it's essential to understand that failure is not a reflection of our personal worth or abilities. Rather, it's an opportunity to learn and grow.

One way to start embracing failure is to practice reframing our perception of it. Instead of viewing failure as a negative outcome, we can reframe it as a learning experience. This shift in perspective allows us to approach setbacks with curiosity and an open mind, rather than fear and shame.

It's also helpful to reflect on past failures and identify the lessons learned. This process can be a valuable exercise in self-reflection and personal growth. Additionally, seeking feedback and constructive criticism can provide valuable insights and areas for improvement.

Finally, it's essential to remember that failure is a natural part of life, and everyone experiences it at some point. By embracing failure and learning from setbacks, we can build resilience and confidence, ultimately leading to a more empowered and fulfilling life as an introvert.

The Power of Self-Acceptance for Introverts

Recognizing and Celebrating Your Unique Qualities

As introverts, we often feel that we don't fit into the standard mold of societal norms. Our quiet nature can sometimes lead us to believe that there's something wrong with us, or that we're not as talented or successful as our more outgoing peers. But the truth is, introverts are gifted with unique qualities that are essential to personal and professional success.

In this section, we'll explore the importance of recognizing and celebrating your unique qualities as an introvert. We'll delve into the science behind introversion and highlight the strengths that come naturally to introverts.

First, let's discuss the various strengths that introverts possess. Introverts are often excellent listeners, able to engage in deep conversations and offer thoughtful insights. They are naturally reflective and introspective, able to process thoughts and emotions deeply. These traits allow introverts to be exceptional problem-solvers, decision-makers, and strategists.

It's also important to recognize that introverts thrive in environments that allow them time to recharge and reflect. Social situations can be draining for introverts, but this doesn't mean that they don't enjoy or value connections with others. Rather, introverts flourish in one-on-one or small group settings that allow for more intimate and meaningful conversations.

Next, let's discuss the importance of embracing your unique qualities as an introvert. By accepting your introverted nature, you can start to recognize and leverage your strengths to achieve success in all areas of your life. Here are a few strategies that can help you embrace your unique qualities:

Focus on your strengths: Identify the traits that come naturally to you as an introvert and focus on building upon these strengths.

Practice self-awareness: Pay attention to your thoughts and emotions and learn to recognize when you're feeling drained or overwhelmed. This will allow you to take steps to recharge and recover before burning out.

Set boundaries: Introverts need time to recharge and reflect, so it's essential to set boundaries in your personal and professional life. This might mean saying no to social events that don't align with your values, or asking for alone time to recharge after a long day of work.

By recognizing and celebrating your unique qualities as an introvert, you'll be able to embrace your introverted nature with confidence and thrive in all areas of your life.

Quieting Your Inner Critic and Practicing Self-Compassion

As introverts, we tend to be our own harshest critics. Our natural inclination towards self-reflection and introspection can sometimes lead us down the path of negative self-talk and self-doubt. We may find ourselves obsessing over past mistakes or worrying excessively about future outcomes, all while criticizing ourselves for not being more outgoing or assertive like our extroverted counterparts. However, self-criticism is not only unhelpful, but it can also be damaging to our mental health and wellbeing. To combat this negative self-talk, it's essential to learn how to practice self-compassion and quiet our inner critic.

Self-compassion is a concept that involves treating ourselves with kindness, understanding, and empathy when we experience pain, failure, or other forms of suffering. It's about learning to accept ourselves for who we are and being our own biggest cheerleader. Research has shown that self-compassion can lead to greater well-being, increased motivation, and more positive overall psychological functioning.

One way to practice self-compassion is to start nurturing a positive internal dialogue. Notice when your inner critic starts to chime in and take a moment to pause and reframe the negative self-talk. Ask yourself what you would say to a friend who shared the same concern or worry. Chances are, you would offer words of encouragement, support, and understanding. It's important to extend the same kindness and compassion to ourselves as we do to others.

Another way to practice self-compassion is to practice mindfulness. Mindfulness involves being present in the moment without judgment or preconceived notions. It can help us to step back from our negative thoughts and emotions and observe them from a more objective stance. By doing so, we can begin to recognize that our thoughts and feelings are not always accurate reflections of reality. We can then learn to let go of negative self-talk and replace it with more positive and affirming self-talk.

Cultivating self-compassion and learning to quiet our inner critic is essential for personal growth and resilience as introverts. By treating ourselves with kindness and empathy, we can build a stronger sense of self-acceptance and inner confidence.

Cultivating Strong, Healthy Relationships with Others

As introverts, we often prefer solitude to social interaction. However, humans are social creatures and we all benefit from meaningful relationships with others. The idea that introverts don't like people is a common misconception that we have already addressed in this book. We simply prefer to interact with people in smaller, more intimate groups or one-on-one.

The key to cultivating strong and healthy relationships with others is to understand and accept ourselves first. When we know who we are and what we need, we can communicate those needs to others and establish boundaries that are healthy for us. Self-acceptance also helps us to be more authentic in our interactions with others, which leads to deeper and more fulfilling relationships.

Another important aspect of cultivating relationships as introverts is to find common ground with others. This can be done by seeking out shared interests or experiences. When we focus on commonalities, we can build connections that transcend our preferences for solitude or social interaction.

Introverts also excel at deep listening, which is a skill that is valued in any relationship. When we are present and actively listening to others, we can form stronger connections and gain a deeper understanding of the people in our lives.

In addition to these strategies, it's important for introverts to take breaks when needed. Social interaction can be draining, and it's vital to take time for ourselves to recharge our batteries. By actively prioritizing self-care, we can show up as our best selves in our relationships with others.

Cultivating strong, healthy relationships as introverts is about finding a balance between social interaction and solitude, being authentic and true to ourselves, and actively prioritizing self-care. When we do this, we can build deep and meaningful connections with others that enrich our lives.

Developing a Personal Support System to Draw on in Times of Stress

As an introvert, you may sometimes feel overwhelmed by the demands of the world around you. It's essential to have a support system in place to help you cope during times of stress. Whether it's a close friend, family member, or support group, having people in your corner can make all the difference.

One important aspect of building a support system is identifying the people in your life who are supportive and understanding of your introverted nature. Look for people who respect your need for alone time and who validate your emotions and experiences. These individuals can help you to feel accepted and understood when you're feeling down.

It's also important to have a variety of coping mechanisms at your disposal. You might try journaling, meditation, or exercise to help manage stress when things get overwhelming. By experimenting with different strategies, you can identify which ones work best for you and incorporate them into your regular self-care routine.

Finally, remember that it's okay to seek professional support when you need it. A therapist can help you work through your emotions and develop coping strategies that work specifically for you. Don't be afraid to reach out for help when you need it - it's a sign of strength, not weakness.

As an introvert, building a support system may take time and effort, but it's well worth the investment. By nurturing personal connections and developing effective coping strategies, you can foster resilience and confidence that will serve you well on your journey to an empowered introverted life.

Setting Boundaries and Prioritizing Your Needs as an Introvert

As an introvert, it can be challenging to set boundaries and prioritize your needs in a world that values extroverted behavior. However, doing so is crucial for maintaining your mental and emotional well-being. In this subsection, we will discuss some strategies you can use to set boundaries and prioritize your needs as an introvert.

One of the first steps in setting boundaries is to be aware of your own limitations. Understanding what drains your energy and what replenishes it can help you manage your time and interactions more effectively. For example, if you find that loud, crowded events are particularly draining for you, it may be helpful to limit your attendance at such events, or to plan ahead to ensure that you have time to recharge afterward.

Another important aspect of setting boundaries is learning to say no. As introverts, we may feel pressured to say yes to social invitations or professional opportunities even when we don't really want to. However, saying yes to everything can lead to burnout and resentment. It's okay to decline invitations or opportunities that don't align with your values or priorities.

Prioritizing your needs also involves taking time for self-care. This can include activities such as taking a quiet walk, reading a book, or practicing meditation. It's important to carve out time in your schedule for activities that nourish your soul and help you feel grounded and centered.

Finally, remember that setting boundaries and prioritizing your needs is not selfish. It's an important aspect of self-care that allows you to show up fully in your relationships, work, and other areas of your life. By setting boundaries and prioritizing your needs, you can cultivate a sense of inner peace and confidence that will serve you well in all aspects of your life.

Chapter 10: Conclusion: The Journey Continues – Your Path to an Empowered Introverted Life

Embracing Your Introverted Nature

Understanding the Benefits of Being Introverted

As we come to the end of our journey together, it's important to reflect on the valuable insights and skills you've gained as an introvert. Throughout this book, we've explored how introverts can excel in a world that often values extroverted qualities. We've debunked stereotypes and misconceptions about introversion, and highlighted unique strengths that introverts possess.

Now, as you continue on your path to an empowered introverted life, it's important to embrace and fully understand the benefits of being introverted. Introverts are known for their deep thinking, introspection, and ability to focus on complex tasks. They often have rich inner worlds and appreciate solitary activities such as reading, writing, or simply reflecting.

In a world that often values constant stimulation and rapid-fire decision making, introverts bring a much-needed balance. They can see the big picture, evaluate options carefully, and come up with creative solutions to complex problems. Introverts have the ability to listen deeply and understand others on a profound level, making them great listeners and empathetic friends.

By embracing your introverted nature and understanding the unique strengths that come with it, you can begin to carve out a fulfilling and empowered life for yourself. Don't let societal pressures push you into behaving in ways that don't feel authentic or natural to you. Instead, embrace your introversion and use it as a source of strength and power. Remember, being an introvert is something to be celebrated, not ashamed of. The world needs your unique perspective and insights – go out there and make your mark!

Overcoming Negative Self-Talk

As an introvert, you may have struggled with negative self-talk throughout your life. Whether it's feeling like you're not good enough or not being able to speak up in a group setting, these thoughts can hold you back from living a fulfilling life.

But it's important to recognize that these thoughts are not reality. They are simply thoughts that have been ingrained in your mind over time. By acknowledging this, you can start to challenge these thoughts and replace them with positive affirmations.

One technique is to write down your negative thoughts and then write a counter-argument to them. For example, if you're feeling like you're not good enough to succeed in a new job, write down why that's not true – perhaps you have relevant experience or a strong work ethic.

It's also important to surround yourself with positive influences, whether it's through supportive friends or inspiring role models. Reading stories about successful introverts can be especially helpful in overcoming negative self-talk.

Finally, remember to practice self-care and prioritize your wellbeing. This can include taking time for yourself to recharge, engaging in activities you enjoy, and seeking professional support when needed. By taking care of yourself and challenging negative self-talk, you can continue on your path towards an empowered introverted life.

Owning Your Unique Perspective

As an introvert, you possess a unique perspective that can help you achieve success in your personal and professional life. Owning your unique perspective means accepting who you are and understanding that your introverted nature provides you with a valuable set of strengths, including your ability to be introspective, empathetic, and focused.

To own your unique perspective, start by recognizing your strengths and how they can benefit you and others. Consider the times when your introverted nature has allowed you to excel, such as when you have been able to solve a complex problem through careful analysis or provide a thoughtful response to an important question.

It is also important to acknowledge any challenges you may

face as an introvert, whether it be anxiety in social situations or difficulty networking. By understanding these challenges, you can work to find strategies that help you overcome them and leverage your strengths to achieve your goals.

Another way to own your unique perspective is by finding your niche. Consider areas where your strengths can be of particular value, such as in roles that require focus and attention to detail or in fields where introverted qualities are highly valued, such as academia or research.

Finally, remember that owning your unique perspective is not about trying to change who you are. Instead, it is about embracing your introverted nature and using it to your advantage. By doing so, you can lead an empowered introverted life and achieve fulfillment and success on your own terms.

Honoring Your Need for Solitude

As an introvert, it is essential to recognize and respect your need for solitude. Solitude provides an opportunity to recharge, reflect, and create, enabling you to be your most authentic and productive self. This is not to say that social interaction is not vital, but rather, it should be balanced with solitary reflection.

When you give yourself permission to embrace solitude, you open yourself up to new experiences and opportunities for growth. Solitude allows you to reflect on your core values, goals, and aspirations without the noise and distractions of the world around you.

Incorporating solitude into your routine may be difficult, especially if you are accustomed to constant stimulation. It is essential to start small and work your way up, setting aside quiet time for yourself each day. This could be as simple as taking a walk in nature or setting aside time to read a book.

Remember, solitude is not isolation. It is essential to foster positive and meaningful relationships in your life while still honoring your need for alone time. By learning to appreciate and embrace solitude, you unlock the potential to live a more authentic and empowered life.

Cultivating Inner Peace and Calm

As an introvert, the path to an empowered life may seem daunting at times. But by embracing your introverted nature, you have already taken the crucial first step towards living a more fulfilling life. In this chapter, we will explore how you can continue to cultivate your inner peace and calm, and how it can positively impact your life.

As an introvert, you are naturally drawn to peaceful and quiet environments. While the outside world may be chaotic, you can find solace in cultivating inner peace and calmness. This can be achieved through practices such as meditation, yoga, or simply taking a walk in nature. By creating moments of stillness in your day, you can recharge your batteries and maintain a sense of calm throughout the day.

Additionally, practicing mindfulness can help you stay present and focused on the task at hand. Mindfulness allows you to observe your thoughts and emotions without judgment, which can help you manage stress and anxiety more effectively. By practicing mindfulness regularly, you can prevent yourself from becoming overwhelmed by external stressors.

Another way to cultivate inner peace and calm is by setting boundaries. As an introvert, you may find yourself saying yes to things you don't want to do, simply because you don't want to disappoint others. However, learning to say no and setting boundaries is an important way to protect your energy and prioritize your needs. By setting clear boundaries, you can create a sense of stability and control in your life, which can help you maintain a sense of calm.

Cultivating inner peace and calm is a crucial aspect of the introverted journey. By practicing mindfulness, setting boundaries, and creating moments of stillness, you can continue to embrace your introverted nature and live a fulfilling life. Remember that this is a journey, and there may be setbacks along the way. But with patience, dedication, and a commitment to your own well-being, you can continue to grow and thrive as an introvert.

Building Strong Relationships as an Introvert

Communicating Effectively with Friends and Family

As an introvert, it can be challenging to communicate effectively with friends and family, especially in large gatherings or social situations. However, it is essential to maintain strong relationships with the people you care about.

One way to communicate more effectively is to focus on quality over quantity. As an introvert, you may not have the energy to engage in small talk or long conversations. Instead, make an effort to have meaningful conversations when you do interact with your loved ones. Ask questions, listen attentively and share your own thoughts and feelings.

Another tip is to set boundaries around your communication needs. Let your friends and family know that you may need alone time to recharge and that it is not a reflection of your feelings towards them. Be clear about your communication preferences, whether it's through phone calls, text messages, or in-person meetings, and find a way that works for everyone involved.

Finally, don't forget to take care of yourself. Self-care is critical for introverts to maintain a healthy balance in their relationships. Make time for solo activities that bring you joy, such as reading a book, taking a walk or indulging in your hobbies. By prioritizing your needs and communicating effectively, you can build and maintain strong relationships with your loved ones.

Networking and Meeting New People as an Introvert

Networking and meeting new people can be particularly challenging for introverts, but it's an essential part of building strong relationships. Here are some introvert-friendly strategies to make networking a more comfortable and rewarding experience:

Set realistic expectations: As an introvert, you may not have the same level of energy and enthusiasm for large social events as your extroverted counterparts. Instead, start small with one-on-one meetings or attending events that interest you.

Come prepared: Before attending an event or meeting, do your homework. Research the attendees, the event's schedule, and topics to anticipate potential conversations.

Listen actively: Introverts are often great listeners, and this is a key asset when networking. Engage in active listening, ask thoughtful questions, and show interest in other people's stories and experiences.

Take breaks: Don't force yourself to stay on when you've already exceeded your social quota. Take breaks when necessary to recharge, and remember that it's okay to excuse yourself politely from a conversation.

Follow up: After meeting new people, follow up with them soon after to continue building your relationships. Introverts often thrive in one-on-one settings, so suggest catching up over coffee or lunch.

By using these strategies, you can network and meet new people in a way that works for you, building strong relationships that support your personal and professional growth as an introvert.

Finding Your Tribe: Connecting with Like-Minded Individuals

As an introvert, building meaningful connections and relationships can be a challenging task. However, it's essential to understand that there are other like-minded individuals out there looking for genuine connections. In this section, we'll discuss how to find your tribe and connect with people who share your interests and values.

Identify your interests and passions

The first step in finding your tribe is identifying your interests and passions. This will help you narrow down your search and connect with people who share similar interests. Take some time to reflect on what you enjoy doing, and jot down a few notes about your passions.

Attend events and gatherings

Once you've identified your interests, attending events and gatherings related to those interests is an excellent way to connect with like-minded individuals. Look for local events and gatherings in your community, and be sure to attend with an open mind and a willingness to meet new people.

Join online groups and communities

In today's digital age, there are countless online groups and communities for every interest and hobby imaginable. Joining these groups can be a great way to connect with others who share your interests, even if they're not local to you. Take the time to explore different online communities, and don't be afraid to reach out and start a conversation.

Volunteer

Volunteering for a cause you care about is not only an excellent way to give back, but it's also an opportunity to connect with like-minded individuals who share your values. Look for volunteer opportunities related to your interests, and take the time to get to know the other volunteers.

Be yourself

Above all, it's important to be yourself when connecting with others. Trying to be someone you're not will only lead to frustration and disappointment in the long run. Embrace your unique qualities and interests, and remember that there are people out there who will appreciate and value them.

By taking these steps to find your tribe and connect with like-minded individuals, you can build strong, meaningful relationships that will support and empower you along your journey as an introvert.

Building Meaningful Relationships

As an introvert, building meaningful relationships can be deeply rewarding and fulfilling, but it can also be challenging. Introverts tend to value deep, authentic connections over superficial interactions, which means that we may struggle in social situations that feel shallow or insincere.

Despite these challenges, however, introverts are uniquely equipped to build strong relationships. Our ability to listen deeply, empathize with others, and reflect on our own thoughts and feelings can make us excellent friends, partners, and colleagues.

If you're an introvert looking to build meaningful relationships, here are some tips to get you started:

Choose your social activities wisely. As an introvert, you're better off focusing your energy on activities that align with your interests and values. This will not only help you meet like-minded people, but it will also make social interactions more enjoyable and meaningful.

Be intentional about your interactions. Rather than trying to be all things to all people, focus on building a few deeper connections. Listen actively, ask questions, share your own experiences, and look for opportunities to support and encourage those around you.

Embrace vulnerability. Building meaningful relationships requires a certain level of vulnerability. Be willing to share your own thoughts, feelings, and experiences, even if it feels uncomfortable at first. It may take time to build trust, but vulnerability is often the key to deepening connections.

Practice self-care. Building meaningful relationships requires energy and emotional investment, so it's important to take care of yourself along the way. Make time for solitude, exercise, healthy meals, and other activities that recharge your batteries and help you stay grounded.

Remember, building meaningful relationships as an introvert is not about trying to be someone you're not. Instead, it's about leveraging your unique strengths and qualities to connect with others in a deeper, more authentic way. By focusing on your values, being intentional about your interactions, and embracing vulnerability and self-care, you can build strong, meaningful relationships that enrich your life and the lives of those around you.

Navigating Romantic Relationships as an Introvert

As an introvert, building strong relationships can be challenging. However, it is crucial to have a fulfilling life. This section focuses on romantic relationships and providing tips for introverts to navigate them successfully.

One of the biggest challenges for introverts in romantic relationships is finding a balance between alone time and time with their partner. It can be difficult for introverts to express their need for alone time without making their partner feel unimportant or neglected. One solution is to communicate openly and honestly with your partner about your needs and find a compromise that works for both of you.

Another challenge for introverts in romantic relationships is dealing with social events and large gatherings. It's not uncommon for introverts to feel drained and overwhelmed after a long day of socializing. In this case, it's important to set boundaries and communicate your needs with your partner. You can try to negotiate, attend events together and set time limits.

It is very important to make sure your partner understands your introvert nature so that they don't mistake your need for alone time as a lack of interest in them. Communication is key here.

Lastly, introverts can benefit from taking the time to choose partners who align with their values, interests, and lifestyle. This may involve some extra effort on their part, but it can lead to a relationship that supports and enhances their introverted nature.

Introverts face unique challenges in romantic relationships, but these challenges can be overcome with communication, setting boundaries, and choosing the right partner. By being mindful of your individual needs and desires, you can build strong and fulfilling romantic relationships while embracing your introverted nature.

Taking Action and Living a Fulfilling Life

Setting Goals and Taking Action towards Your Dreams

As an introvert, it can be easy to let life pass you by. You may have a strong desire to achieve your dreams and goals, but struggle to take action towards them. In this final section, we will delve into the importance of setting goals and taking action, and how it can lead to a more fulfilling life.

Setting goals is an essential part of personal growth and development. By setting clear and concise goals, you give yourself something specific to work towards. It's crucial to make sure these goals are SMART - specific, measurable, attainable, relevant, and time-bound. This will help you create a clear plan of action.

Once you've set your goals, the next step is taking action. Avoid getting stuck in analysis paralysis, and instead, take small steps towards achieving your goals every day. By breaking down large tasks into smaller, manageable ones, you'll be more likely to follow through with them.

While taking action towards achieving your goals is essential, remember to be kind to yourself in the process. Don't let setbacks discourage you, but instead, view them as opportunities to learn and grow. Celebrate your successes along the way, no matter how small they may seem.

Setting goals and taking action towards achieving them is a

crucial part of living a fulfilling life as an introvert. By doing so, you can create a life that aligns with your desires and aspirations, and not let your introverted nature hold you back. Remember, the journey towards personal growth and development is ongoing, so keep setting new goals and taking action towards achieving them.

Celebrating Your Successes and Learning from Your Failures

As an introvert, it's important to recognize your achievements and celebrate your successes. Take time to reflect on what you have accomplished, no matter how small or insignificant it may seem. You deserve credit for your hard work and dedication.

At the same time, it's essential to acknowledge and learn from your failures. It's easy to get discouraged by setbacks and feel like giving up, but remember that failure is a natural part of the learning process. Instead of dwelling on your mistakes, try to see them as opportunities for growth and learning.

One effective way to celebrate your successes and learn from your failures is to keep a journal. Write down your achievements and failures, along with a brief summary of what you learned from each experience. This can help you stay motivated and focused on your goals, as well as provide valuable insight into your strengths and weaknesses.

Another strategy is to surround yourself with supportive people who can offer encouragement and advice. Find trusted mentors or friends who believe in your abilities and can help you navigate the ups and downs of pursuing your passions.

Remember, success is not a destination but rather a journey. It's important to enjoy the ride and appreciate the progress you make along the way. With determination and perseverance, you can continue to achieve success and live a fulfilling and empowered introverted life.

Prioritizing Self-Care and Wellbeing

As an introvert, it's important that you prioritize self-care and wellbeing to stay balanced and energized. Here are some strategies to help you take care of yourself and lead a fulfilling life:

Embrace solitude: As an introvert, you thrive in quiet and reflective moments. Make sure to carve out time for yourself each day to recharge and rejuvenate. This could be anything from reading a book to taking a hot bath or going for a walk in nature.

Focus on your physical health: Your physical health plays a key role in your mental and emotional wellbeing. Make sure to prioritize exercise, healthy eating, and getting enough sleep to optimize your overall health.

Practice mindfulness: Mindfulness can help you stay grounded and present in the moment, reducing stress and anxiety. Try practicing meditation or deep breathing exercises to help you stay centered throughout the day.

Set boundaries: As an introvert, you may struggle with

saying no and setting boundaries. However, it's important to prioritize your own needs and not overextend yourself. Learn to say no when you need to and set limits on your time and energy.

Pursue your passions: To live a fulfilling life, it's important to pursue your passions and hobbies. Make sure to carve out time for the things you love and prioritize your own interests and goals.

Remember, prioritizing self-care and wellbeing is not selfish, but rather essential for leading a healthy and fulfilling life as an introvert. By taking care of yourself, you can show up as your best self in both your personal and professional life.

Embracing and Overcoming Challenges

Introduction:

In the previous chapters, we've talked about introversion, the science behind it, and ways to thrive as an introvert in an extroverted world. Now, in this final chapter, we'll discuss taking action and living a fulfilling life as an empowered introvert. It's time to put all the knowledge and strategies we've learned into practice.
Being an introvert comes with its own set of challenges. Perhaps you've struggled with public speaking, networking, or being assertive in social or professional settings. It's essential to remember that these challenges are not unique to introverts, and they can be overcome.

One way to embrace and overcome challenges is by stepping outside your comfort zone. As an introvert, you might be more comfortable in solitary activities, such as reading or hiking. However, challenging yourself to engage in social events or speaking opportunities can help you build resilience and self-confidence. Start small and work your way up to higher-stake situations.

Another way to overcome challenges is by reframing your mindset. Instead of thinking of networking or public speaking as draining or anxiety-inducing, try to view them as growth opportunities. Recognize that everyone experiences nerves or discomfort at times, and that's okay. Reframing your mindset can help you approach these situations with a more positive and empowered attitude.

It's also important to identify and leverage your strengths. Remember, introverts have unique strengths that can be valuable in various contexts. By identifying your strengths, such as active listening or attention to detail, you can highlight them in social or professional settings to showcase your unique value.

Ultimately, overcoming challenges as an introvert takes practice and patience. But by embracing and challenging yourself, reframing your mindset, and leveraging your strengths, you can live a more fulfilling and empowered life as an introvert.

Continuing Your Personal Growth Journey as an Empowered Introvert

As an introvert, personal growth is an ongoing journey of self-discovery and self-improvement. It requires a commitment to your own personal development and a willingness to step out of your comfort zone. Here are some tips on how to continue your personal growth journey as an empowered introvert:

Prioritize self-care: Make sure you are taking care of your physical and mental health. This includes getting enough sleep, eating well, exercising regularly, and taking time for relaxation and self-reflection.

Embrace new experiences: While it's important to honor your introverted nature and take time to recharge, don't shy away from new experiences that challenge you and help you grow. This could be something as simple as trying a new hobby or taking a class.

Practice mindfulness: Being present in the moment and mindful of your thoughts and emotions can help you better understand yourself and cultivate a sense of inner peace and calm. Consider incorporating practices like meditation or journaling into your daily routine.

Set goals: Identify what you want to achieve and set specific, measurable goals to get there. This will help you stay focused and motivated on your personal growth journey.

Surround yourself with supportive people: Seek out relationships with people who support your personal growth and understand and respect your introverted nature. This might include finding a mentor or joining a community of like-minded individuals.

Remember, personal growth is a lifelong journey, and there is no "right" way to do it. Stay true to yourself, honor your introverted nature, and be open to new experiences and opportunities for growth. With time and dedication, you can continue to develop into an empowered introvert who embraces your strengths and confidently navigates the world around you.

oduct-compliance